IN COMMUNION

WITH CHRIST

IN COMMUNION
WITH CHRIST

Jose and Dalia Licea

Christian
Catholic Media
PRESS

Published by
Christian Catholic Media
Visalia, California
ChristianCatholicMedia.com
1st edition, June 2021
Printed in the United States of America

ISBN
Hardcover ISBN: 978-1-7374137-0-7
Paperback ISBN: 978-1-7374137-1-4
e-book ISBN: 978-1-7374137-2-1
Audiobook ISBN: 978-1-7374137-3-8

This book is dedicated to our children.

TABLE OF CONTENTS

INTRODUCTION

When I was fifteen years old, my father was diagnosed with cancer. I knew he would make it. I knew he would survive. Five years later, everything was forever changed.

I was on the plane home from Las Vegas, Nevada when it occurred to me that nothing would ever be the same. My father as I had always known him, was no longer. This was apparent after this visit I had with him, pushing him along in his wheelchair with his oxygen tanks, to get a glimpse of the Grand Canyon. It was a breathtaking sight but it felt very surreal given the circumstances.

Even if his health improved, he would never quite be the same after everything he had been through. He could no longer use his hands to play the guitar, a pastime he so dearly loved. He could barely hold his breath long enough to sing, and he struggled to walk due to inflammation from his failing organs. For some odd reason, I still had faith that he would survive but in the pit of my stomach, I knew that even though he was still alive, he was in unbearable pain and his joy was lost.

When the plane landed back in California, my maternal grandfather greeted me at the airport. We started the drive home and I called my father to let him know I had arrived safely and was in the car on my way home with my grandfather. I don't think he understood much of what I was saying to him at the time. He sounded pretty out of it from all of the pain medication he was taking. Just before we got off the phone, I said to him, "I love you, dad."

In a moment of clarity, he responded, "I love you too."

Then the call ended.

The next day was October 31, 2003. I was in my first year of college after spending a year abroad as an exchange student in Argentina. I was twenty years old. I had a scheduled interview for the teacher preparation program at the college I was attending and just as I had finished getting ready for my interview, the phone rang. It was George. George was a longtime friend of my father and the person my father had been staying with for some time while he was really sick. As soon as I said hello, I heard George's voice say, "He's gone."

There is something about that moment when you hear those words that I'll never forget. Emotions rush over you like nothing you have ever experienced before. The sting of loss is a fiery one. It takes hold of you and tears burst out of your eyes like a tidal wave. Nothing can hold them back. George was a grown man bawling like a baby right along with me. Neither one of us could say much at that point and so he handed the phone to the hospice nurse. She was very skilled at her job. She said very comforting words to me to try and calm my soul. I could tell she had been through this before. She reassured me that he looked very peaceful. His pain was gone. So much for my interview. I knew there was no way that was going to happen that day. I was in too much shock from the news of my loss.

My automatic next move was to call my boyfriend (now husband) named Jose Licea. I just remember feeling a dire need to have him there quickly. I was all alone and I had just received the worst news I had ever received in my entire life. I needed somebody to be with me and he was the one. Thankfully, he arrived swiftly. I then called my mother to tell her what happened, and she rushed home early from work as well. Then the three of us were on our way to a small city just outside of Las Vegas, called Pahrump, Nevada. I had to say my goodbyes one last time.

My father was raised in a Catholic home. His mother (my grandmother whom I had never met because she had passed before I was born) sang in the choir at her local parish. My aunt often told me about my grandmother playing the piano every day. Music was in her soul. She must be the root of my father's musical talents. Unfortunately, my father drifted from his faith during his teenage years as so many often do. He only returned to Mass with me a few times during the last year of his life. He may never have gone back to Mass before taking his last breath if I had never met Jose and began my journey with the Catholic faith.

I was not raised as a Catholic. My parents divorced when I was very young. During my upbringing, my father was no longer practicing his Catholic faith and was living a secular life. My mother had become a Christian (Protestant) as a young adult so I was raised in various Protestant and non-denominational church settings. I may have never become Catholic if it were not for meeting my husband who also almost fell away from the faith at one point when his siblings were turning to Protestantism in its various forms but his mother persisted in prayer (I am sure) and so began his quest for truth. He has spent the last couple of decades of his life studying Christianity and the critical role that is played by the Catholic Church in our short journey here on earth. He has discovered many truths as have many other Catholics on this same quest. Along the quest for truth, there is much adversity and truth must always be defended.

The defense of Catholic truth is known as Catholic apologetics. This does not mean apologizing like saying that you are sorry for something. The term, apologetics, refers to the branch of theology that defends the faith against objections. This book is not about apologetics (That will be left for another book). This book is about living a life in communion with Christ. It is about exploring the gifts we have here on this earth from Christ within the Catholic Church. These gifts are made known to us from promises in scripture and in Catholic traditions. It could be argued that the Bible as we know it today is a Catholic tradition in and of itself since the canon comes directly from councils held by the Catholic Church but that is a separate topic best kept for another book.

What does it mean to live a life in communion with Christ? It means living a life where at our end of days, our Father in Heaven, invites us into His kingdom with open arms. It means embracing God's call to accept His grace and all of its transformational power. The Catholic Church is God's gift to all people who will accept it and is filled with many more mysterious gifts to assist us in accepting God's grace. If you would like to live a life in communion with Christ, then this book was written for you. The format of this book is more like a course in accepting God's graces and gifts. Each chapter is written like a study unit broken into subtopics. The topic of each chapter is first introduced and then each subtopic is explored and followed by a section of beautiful words from a Saint who has ultimately lived his or her own life in communion with Christ and whose example we have to follow. You will then be called to reflect on a way that you can respond to God's call in your life. Following each reflection is a prayer that you can pray in sincerity to God and move you to take the next step in living your life in communion with Christ.

1 THE MASS

- *What is the Mass?*
- *The Significance of the Eucharist*
- *Christ's Presence Among Us*
- *God's Channel of Grace to the World*
- *Origins of the Mass*
- *Eucharistic Adoration*
- *A Foretaste of Heaven*

When a person thinks of the Catholic Mass, he might envision a structured ceremony in a grand church, accented by rays of light streaming through stained-glass windows upon clouds of incense. He might think of the priest raising the bread and wine at the altar while the congregation kneels in reverent prayer. He might think of a joyous midnight Christmas concert with trumpets proclaiming the birth of the Messiah, or a solemn Easter vigil with the faithful processing their small candles into a dark church. The Mass is all these things and more.

To understand the Mass is to understand the very heart of Catholicism. The Mass is the ritual whereby Christ's sacrifice is re-presented to the faithful. It is how Jesus fulfills his promise to be always among us. Indeed, it is through the celebration of the Mass and Jesus' Divine Presence in the Holy Eucharist that God remains visible, accessible, and available to humanity.

What is the Mass?

Simply put, the Mass is the Sacrament of the Eucharist. More than just a church service, the Mass presents an outward sign of inward grace—God's life offered for us. During the Mass, the priest consecrates bread and wine which become the Divine Body and Blood of Jesus. The faithful partake of this sacrament in Holy Communion— uniting themselves wholly to Jesus.

For those seeking adoption into God's family, the Sacrament of Communion completes the process of initiation for all baptized persons. Through partaking in this Divine Bread and Wine, those who have already been baptized, "participate with the whole community in the Lord's own sacrifice by means of the Eucharist" (CCC 1322).

The Catholic faith places utmost importance on the Mass, as the Eucharist "is the source and summit of the Christian life" (1324). All other sacraments—baptism, reconciliation, confirmation, holy matrimony and holy orders, as well as last rites—intertwine with the celebration of the Holy Eucharist. They point to the Eucharist and stem from the Divine Sacrament because in this small host "is contained the whole spiritual good of the Church, namely Christ himself," our Paschal Lamb (CCC 1324).

Priests and clerics "are especially bound to pursue holiness because they are consecrated to God.... In order for them to pursue this perfection, ...they are to nourish their spiritual life from the two-fold table of Sacred Scripture and the Eucharist; priests are therefore earnestly invited to offer the sacrifice of the Eucharist daily..." (Code of Canon Law #276). Therefore, partaking in daily Mass is desirable for any person who wishes to pursue perfection of the soul.

Most Catholic churches offer Mass for the faithful every day of the week year round (except for Good Friday, during which the Church offers a Communion service — distribution of pre-consecrated Eucharist).

One of the greatest marks of a saintly soul is regular and diligent devotion to the Holy Mass. St. Therese of Lisieux declared that "The best means to reach perfection is through receiving Holy Communion frequently. Experience sufficiently proves it in those who practice it." Receiving our Lord in the Eucharist in this life is the surest guarantee of joining Him in that the next life, where Christ longingly awaits us.

What Do the Saints Say?

ST. CYRIL OF JERUSALEM wrote clearly and simply on the Holy Eucharist during the 4th century. He shows us the staunch faith of the early Church in the anointed authority of the priesthood and its power to transform bread and wine into the living Jesus Christ. In the Church's earliest days, faith in the Holy Eucharist as the living Christ has been

7

continuous, as is shown in Cyril's writing.

The bread and wine of the Eucharist before the invocation of the holy and adorable Trinity were simply bread and wine. But after the invocation, the bread becomes the Body of Christ and the wine becomes the Blood of Christ (Catechetical Discourses, 19,7).

Therefore, what starts as mere bread and wine is altered by the priest during Mass into the Body and Blood of Our Lord.

Reflection

How can I make the Mass more central to my Christian lifestyle?

Time For Prayer

Anima Christi

Soul of Christ, sanctify me;
Body of Christ, save me;
Blood of Christ, inebriate me;
Water from the side of Christ, wash me;
Passion of Christ, strengthen me;
O good Jesus hear me;
Within your wounds hide me; separated
from you, let me never be; From the evil
one protect me;
At the hour of my death, call me;

And close to you bid me; That with your saints, I
may be praising you forever and ever.

The Significance of the Eucharist

The Eucharist is essential to Catholic life. As with
anything of high importance and value, it goes by many
names. It is the Heavenly Manna, The Bread of Life, the Body
and Blood of Christ, The Divine Sacrifice, The Real Presence.
It is the Most Blessed Sacrament.

The Holy Eucharist has three profound aspects:

1. It is the Sacrifice Sacrament of the Mass. During the
Mass, Jesus is offered by the priest to Heavenly Father as
the Paschal Lamb—the innocent blood sacrificed for the
sake of our sins.

2. It is the Communion Sacrament of Holy
Communion. During Communion, the faithful are
wholly united to the Divine Jesus. Through this union,
they grow in grace to be more like Christ.

3. It is also the Presence Sacrament. The Eucharist allows
Jesus to be physically present to his followers, thus
fulfilling his promise, "Behold, I am with you always,
even until the end of the age" (Matthew 28:20).

What Do the Saints Say?

ST. THOMAS AQUINAS received orders from the pope in the 11th century to compose hymns for the Divine Office of the Corpus Christi feast. Accordingly, Aquinas composed the Lauda Sion Salvatorem, which offers clear teaching on the Eucharist.

Christ's followers know by faith that bread is changed into His flesh and wine into His blood. Man cannot understand this, cannot perceive it; but a lively faith affirms that the change, which is outside the natural course of things, takes place. Under the different species, which are now signs only and not their own reality, there lie hidden wonderful realities. His body is our food, His blood our drink. And yet Christ remains entire under each species. The communicant receives the complete Christ—uncut, unbroken, and undivided.

Every portion of the Eucharistic Bread and Wine contains the whole of the Soul and Divinity of Our Lord. For He can neither be divided nor diminished.

Reflection

How can we take time to experience the Eucharist as our daily bread?

Time For Prayer

<u>The Divine Praises</u>

Blessed be God.

Blessed be His Holy Name.

Blessed be Jesus Christ, true God and true Man.

Blessed be the Name of Jesus.

Blessed be His Most Sacred Heart.

Blessed be His Most Precious Blood.

Blessed be Jesus in the Most Holy Sacrament of the Altar.

Blessed be the Holy Spirit, the Paraclete.

Blessed be the great Mother of God, Mary most Holy.

Blessed be her Holy and Immaculate Conception.

Blessed be her Glorious Assumption.

Blessed be the name of Mary, Virgin and Mother.

Blessed be St. Joseph, her most chaste spouse.

Blessed be God in His Angels and in His Saints.

Christ's Presence Among Us

The Eucharist is nothing less than the Divine presence of God himself. The substance that begins as basic bread and wine is miraculously transformed into the Body and Blood of our Divine Savior, Jesus Christ. The Eucharist is Christ's personal offering—the gift of his own self. The beauty of such a gift is that it brings forth God's grace into the world. When we partake of the Most Blessed Sacrament, we become vessels of the Divine Presence—we carry Jesus within us. We in turn bring that presence into the rest of the world to each person we meet. Each Mass ends with the priest's proclamation: "The Mass is now ended. Let us go forth to love and serve the world."

What Do the Saints Say?

ST. TERESA OF AVILA wrote in the 16th century about the mystery of the Holy Eucharist. Wholly God and wholly human, Jesus in the Holy Eucharist is most certainly The Mystery of Faith. Teresa wrote about the mystery in this way:

"Once after receiving Communion, I was given an understanding of how the Father receives within our soul the most holy Body of Christ, and of how I know and have seen that these Divine Persons are present, and how pleasing to the Father this offering of His Son is, because He delights and rejoices with Him here—let us say—on earth. For His humanity is not present with us in the soul, but His divinity is. Thus the humanity is so welcome and pleasing to the Father and bestows on us so many favors."

One side of the mystery is that God became man in order to redeem the world by His death. Yet the graces distributed through this offering are not confined the singular event of Christ's Crucifixion on Good Friday. Holy Masses are celebrated each day at different hours around the world. Altogether, they form a continuous sacrifice to God the Father. They offer constant graces which are distributed for us through the substance of the Eucharist.

At the heart of the Catholic faith is the belief that God assumed our human nature so that he could serve as the channel of the graces needed to reach our heavenly destiny. Therefore, the Holy Eucharist acts as the chief channel of the light to illuminate our minds and help us dispel the darkness of our hearts. It is the select source of nourishment—the daily bread—which enables us to bear our daily cross.

Reflection

Knowing that Christ remains present to us in the Holy Eucharist, how can we be more present to Him?

Time For Prayer

Hail to Thee, True Body

(A Prayer to our Eucharistic Lord)

Hail to thee, true body born
From Virgin Mary's womb!
The same that on the cross was nailed
And bore for man the bitter doom.
Thou, whose side was pierced and flowed
Both with water and with blood;
Suffer us to taste of thee,
In our life's last agony.
O kind, O loving one!
O sweet Jesus, Mary's Son!

God's Channel of Grace to the World

Imagine the Eucharist like a divine fire which illuminates our souls. We approach that light and become ignited ourselves. We bring our own flames of light with us into the darkness of the world to cast away the shadows. We offer our lights so that others may also ignite their own flames as well. In this way, we spread Christ's light throughout the world.

The other miracle of the Eucharist is its amazing ability to change us to be more like Christ. With any other food substance, we consume it and it breaks down into basic elements to become more like the substance of our bodies. However, when we consume the Bread of Life, we enter into Communion with Jesus. It alters us so that we become more Christ-like and enables us to better participate as the communal Body of Christ on earth.

What Do the Saints Say?

ST. MARGARET MARY wrote numerous letters in the 17th century to those seeking her counsel. One such letter describes our Lord in the Blessed Sacrament. Margaret Mary wrote the following to help the faithful honor Christ during the Octave of the feast of Corpus Christi.

Today the Lord wants you to honor His life wholly given to us in the Blessed Sacrament. You must be as a burning candle with no other desire than to be consumed in His honor. Surrender yourself to the Mercy of Providence and let Him do with you according to His designs.

When we partake of the Eucharist, we offer ourselves to be transformed by the Lord.

Reflection

In receiving God's sacramental grace, how do we strive to offer that illuminating grace to others?

Time For Prayer
St. John Vianney Prayer

"O my God, come to me, so that You may dwell in me and I may dwell in you."

Origins of the Mass

The Mass originated with Jesus' breaking of the bread with his disciples. When we meditate upon the final luminous mystery of the rosary, The Institution of the Eucharist, our minds dwell on the Last Supper of the Lord. On that Holy Thursday, Jesus commenced His paschal sacrifice, which was not completed until He poured out His lifeblood on the cross. During the Passover feast, Jesus gathered with the apostles in the Upper Room. He "took bread and blessed and broke it and gave it to them and said, 'Take, this is my body.' And He took a cup and when He had given thanks, He gave it to them and they drank all of it and

He said to them, 'This is my blood of the New Covenant which is poured out for many'" (Mark 14:22-24).

What Do the Saints Say?

ST. ALPHONSUS LIGUORI is known for his 18th century work, The Holy Eucharist. He speaks clearly about the Most Blessed Sacrament.

Our holy faith teaches us, and we are bound to believe, that in the consecrated Host, Jesus Christ is really present under the species of bread. But we must also understand that He is thus present on our altars as on a throne of love and mercy, to dispense graces and there to show us the love which He bears us, by being pleased to dwell night and day hidden in the midst of us.

Jesus humbles himself to dwell, hidden and silent, among us. He is present to us always, waiting for us to visit him.

Reflection

How can we understand more deeply the connection between the Passover feast and how Jesus fulfills the Old Testament foreshadowing of Christ as the Paschal Lamb?

Time For Prayer

<u>Short Prayer After Communion</u>

Sweetest Jesus,
Body and Blood most Holy,
be the delight and pleasure of my soul,
my strength and salvation in all temptations,
my joy and peace in every trial,
my light and guide in every word and deed,
my final protection in death. Amen

Eucharistic Adoration

The Eucharist is rightly honored even apart from the Mass. Frequently on holy days or the first Saturday of each month, priests will place the consecrated Host in a precious display case so that Jesus may be adored. The display case is called a monstrance and often resembles a shining sun. The monstrance is made of precious metals and is sometimes embedded with jewels to adorn God in His majesty.

Adoration is commonly preceded by prayers of Benediction, whereby the faithful sing the holy praises of God. The Church has a Rite of Eucharistic Exposition and Benediction which concludes with the ordained minister raising the monstrance and blessing the faithful with the Blessed Sacrament.

At times, the Eucharist in the monstrance is carried by the priest in a procession. The faithful treat this movement of the Lord the way subjects would treat a procession of their king—by reverently kneeling or bowing as the Eucharist passes by. Many graces are bestowed upon all in the presence of the Holy Eucharist, whether during a procession, benediction, or adoration.

What Do the Saints Say?

ST. PETER JULIAN EYMARD organized two congregations in the early 19th century: Congregation of the Blessed Sacrament for men and Servants of the Blessed Sacrament for women. He spoke of the virtues that Our Eucharistic Lord practices in the present, leading us by His example.

Jesus wanted to be the poorest of the poor, in order to be able to stretch out His hand to the lowliest of men and say to them, "I am your brother."

No man, in fact, was ever born in more wretched conditions than the Word Incarnate, who had the litter of animals for His cradle and their shelter for His home.

And now that He is risen and glorious, He still takes poverty for His companion. Jesus, dwelling in our midst in His Sacrament, is poorer than during the days of His mortal life.

His priests or His faithful people must give Him everything; the matter of the sacrament, the bread and the wine; the linen on which to place Him or with which to cover Him; the corporals, the altar cloths. He brings nothing from heaven except his adorable person and His love.

Peter Julian teaches that Jesus Christ is to be imitated in

both aspects of his being: as the God-man who lived a mortal life on earth, and also as the same Word-Made-Flesh who is this very moment living His glorified life in the Blessed Sacrament.

Reflection

How can I more deeply reflect upon Christ as the shining sun bringing warmth, light, and life to my Christian faith?

Time For Prayer

A Short Adoration Prayer Before Meditation

I place myself in the presence of Him, in whose Incarnate Presence I am before. I place myself there.

I adore Thee, O my Savior, present here as God and man, in soul and body, in true flesh and blood.

I acknowledge and confess that I kneel before that Sacred Humanity, which was conceived in Mary's womb and lay in Mary's bosom; which grew up to man's estate, and by the Sea of Galilee called the Twelve, wrought miracles, and spoke words of wisdom and peace; which in due season hung on the cross, lay in the tomb, rose from the dead, and now reigns in heaven.

I praise, and bless, and give myself wholly to Him, Who is the true Bread of my soul, and my everlasting joy.

A Foretaste of Heaven

The glorified Christ dwells among us, particularly in the earthly liturgy of the Mass. Christ remains with His followers "present in his Church, especially in her liturgical celebrations...especially in the Eucharistic species.... He is present in his word since it is he himself who speaks when the holy Scriptures are read in the Church.... The Church is his beloved Bride who calls to her Lord and through him offers worship to the eternal Father" (CCC 1088-1089). The Communion we experience with God through the Mass is but a foretaste of the complete communion we shall experience with God in heaven.

What Do the Saints Say?

ST. THERESE OF LISIEUX during her brief life in the later 19th century once expressed her great joy after receiving Holy Communion in these words:

"It was utterly heavenly happiness, the kind that words cannot express. And what shall our happiness be when we receive Communion in the eternal abode of the King of Heaven? Then we shall see our joy never coming to an end; there will no longer be the sadness of departing, and it will be no longer necessary to have some souvenir to dig fervently into the walls sanctified by His divine presence, for His home will be ours for all eternity."

The Eucharist is both the anticipation and the promise of heaven. In heaven, Christ, who is now hidden in the Blessed

Sacrament, will then be seen face to face.

Reflection

What are we doing today in our daily lives to practice for the complete communion with God which we anticipate in our afterlives?

Time For Prayer

Fatima Angel's Prayer

(Given by an angel to the children of Fatima)

O Most Holy Trinity, Father, Son and Holy Spirit, I adore Thee profoundly. I offer Thee the most precious Body, Blood, Soul and Divinity of Jesus Christ, present in all the tabernacles of the world, in reparation for the outrages, sacrileges and indifference by which He is offended. By the infinite merits of the Sacred Heart of Jesus and the Immaculate Heart of Mary, I beg the conversion of poor sinners.

2 CONFESSION

- *What is Confession?*
- *Why Must We confess to a Priest?*
- *What Should We Confess?*
- *How Reconciliation Brings Us Closer to Christ and the Church*

Confession is shrouded in secrecy and therefore evokes mixed emotions. Movies often portray the sacrament as happening in a tiny cell with a hidden priest leaning toward the penitent who is kneeling in a dark space, whispering into a screen.

Such an intimate occurrence is easily misunderstood. People wonder why confession is necessary, why a person must reveal their sins to a priest, and why the priest is sworn to secrecy. Christ gave the Church the sacrament of Confession as a way to continue the healing of sins. Through Confession, we receive the grace to live virtuously, reconciliation with God, and the healing of relationships we have wounded through our wrong actions.

What is Confession?

Confession is a way to apologize for wrongs and resolve to do better. As it provides many positive ways to assist the faithful, it goes by several names. Confession is the sacrament of conversion, the sacrament of Penance, the sacrament of forgiveness, and the sacrament of reconciliation.

It is commonly called confession because it involves "the disclosure or confession of sins to a priest [as] an essential element of this sacrament. In a profound sense, it is also a "confession"—acknowledgment and praise—of the holiness of God and of his mercy toward sinful man" (CCC 1424). Therefore, through this practice of humility, we admit our wrongdoings, yet we also attest to God's goodness in his glorious mercy towards sinners.

It is the sacrament of conversion because "it makes sacramentally present Jesus' call to conversion, the first step in returning to the Father from whom one has strayed by sin" (CCC 1423). When we sin, we chose a path that moves us away from God. Jesus calls us to move toward the Father. However, the first step in doing that is to change direction— to repent. Conversion cannot take place without a heart of repentance.

This is frequently referred to as the sacrament of Penance since it "consecrates the Christian sinner's personal and ecclesial steps of conversion, penance, and satisfaction" (CCC 1423). Through revealing our sins and voicing them to a priest, we solidify our resolve to repair the damage done in our own lives and the lives of others. This reparation within self and with others leads also to reparation with God.

Penance is an act of atonement prescribed by the priest. This atonement is usually something fitting of the sin confessed. For example, if a person has been unjustly harsh with their children, the penance might be to write notes of praise to the children in an effort to build better family relationships. Or, if a person has been living with a partner outside of marriage, the penance might be to meditate on the story of Jesus's forgiveness of Mary Magdalene. It is important to remember, however, that penance is not a free pass to go return to wrongdoing. To be valid, the sacrament must be made with a sincere resolve to improve one's behavior.

The sacrament is a beloved practice because it grants pardon and peace. Still, the focus should not be entirely on the self as on the relationship it heals. That is why this sacrament is most accurately portrayed in the title, the Sacrament of Reconciliation. Through absolution, the priest "imparts to the sinner the love of God who reconciles: [saying] 'Be reconciled to God'" (CCC 1423).

What Do the Saints Say?

ST. FAUSTINA OF POLAND wrote extensively of God as the Giver of Mercy. In her recommendations for confession, she pointed to pride as the chief obstacle which causes one to hesitate in approaching the confessional.

A soul does not benefit from the sacrament of confession if it is not humble. Pride keeps it in darkness. The soul neither knows how nor is it willing, to probe with precision the depths of its misery. It puts on a mask and avoids everything that might bring it recovery.

In telling one's sins to a priest, a person can receive objective advice on methods to overcome the sin which keeps him from God.

Reflection

How can we examine our conscience to make a sincere confession?

Time For Prayer

Prayer Before Confession

O Holy Spirit. Source of all light, Spirit of wisdom, of understanding, and of knowledge, come to
my assistance and enable me to make a good confession.

Enlighten me and help me now to know my sins as one day I shall be forced to recognize them before Thy
judgment seat.

Bring to my mind the evil which I have done and the good which I have neglected. Permit me not to be blinded
by self- love.

Grant me, moreover, heartfelt sorrow for my

transgressions, and the grace of a sincere confession, so that I may be forgiven and admitted into Thy friendship.

Why Must We Confess to A Priest?

Some of the most common questions about confession are: Why is it necessary to confess to a priest? Doesn't God forgive the sins of any repentant sinner? and Can't we just say a sincere prayer and receive God's grace?

Certainly, we should not limit God's ability to bestow grace. However, Jesus gave specific authority to the apostles, establishing a clear practice and tradition for sacramental reconciliation between man and God.

Firstly, we must establish that only God forgives sins. Jesus confirmed that "the Son of man has authority on earth to forgive sins" (Matthew 9:6). Yet, Christ "entrusted the exercise of the power of absolution to the apostolic ministry which he charged with the 'ministry of reconciliation'" (CCC 1442). Therefore, Jesus handed over the power of absolution to his apostles, and effectively, to the Church through apostolic succession.

Christ solemnly stated: "I will give you the keys of the kingdom of heaven, and whatever you bind on earth shall be bound in heaven, and whatever you lose on earth shall be loosed in heaven" (Matthew 16:19). He voiced this conferral to Simon Peter, however, the charge "was also assigned to the college of the apostles united to [the office of Peter] its head" (CCC 1444). Thus, Christ gave the apostles and each of their successors the authority to either exclude sinners from the Church or welcome them back into the community.

Additionally, Jesus spoke about this special authority after his resurrection when he appeared to the apostles in the Upper Room. In an effort to ease their fear, Jesus said to them, "'Peace be with you. As the Father has sent me, even so I send you. And when he had said this, he breathed on them, and said to them, 'Receive the Holy Spirit. If you forgive the sins of any, they are forgiven; if you retain the sins of any, they are retained'" (John 20:21-23). Jesus commissioned his apostles to leave the Upper Room, go out into the world, and forgive sins in his name. Jesus understood that through such forgiveness, flows peace.

The priest in the confessional acts in persona Christi —in the person of Christ— reconciling the sinner to the Father on behalf of Jesus himself. The sacrament is valid regardless of the priest's virtue. However, the priest has a great responsibility toward holiness if such a sacrament is to be inviting and successful.

Pope Saint John Paul II wrote in his 1984 apostolic exhortation "Reconciliatio et Paenitentia" (Reconciliation and Penance) that each confessor should have the virtues of "prudence, discretion, discernment, a firmness tempered with gentleness and goodness." He should be prepared through studies in "theology, in pedagogy and psychology, in the methodology of dialogue and above all, in the living and communicative knowledge of the word of God." Additionally, the priest's lifestyle should be exemplary in that he should practice "an intense and genuine spiritual life. To lead others into the way of Christian perfection, the ministry of penance should be present in his own life, more by his actions than by words, thus giving proof of a true experience of real prayer, of the practice of the theological and moral virtues, of faithful obedience to the will of God, of love of the Church and of docility to its magisterium."

Let us recall that the essence of a sacrament is to utilize the material, the visible and tangible matter, to be a sign of the spiritual, the invisible and divine grace. Thus, the matter of the sacrament is offered by the penitent: the contrition (sorrow for sins, as evident in the recitation of the Act of Contrition), the confession (in-person verbalization of wrongdoings), and the satisfaction (penance offered in reparation for the damage done).

The priest offers the proper form for the sacrament, saying: "God, the Father of mercies, through the death and resurrection of his Son has reconciled the world to himself and sent the Holy Spirit among us for the forgiveness of sins; through the ministry of the Church, may God give you pardon and peace, and I absolve you from your sins in the name of the Father, and of the Son, and of the Holy Spirit."

What Do the Saints Say?

ST. FRANCIS DE SALES encouraged the faithful to establish a relationship with a trustworthy priest who would guide them in their spiritual journey toward virtuous living.

Go to your confessor; open your heart to him; display to him all the recesses of your soul; take the advice that he will give you with the utmost humility and simplicity. For God, Who has an infinite love for obedience, frequently renders profitable the counsels we take from others, but especially from those who are the guides of our souls.

Once a good confessor is found, it is wise to follow his advice so that we may rid ourselves of anything hindering us from advancing in holiness.

Reflection

How can I establish a habit of the sacrament of Reconciliation?

Time For Prayer

Act of Contrition

O my God, I am heartily sorry for having offended Thee. And I detest all my sins because I dread the loss of heaven and the pains of hell, but most of all because they offend Thee, my God, Who art all good and deserving of all my love.

I firmly resolve, with the help of Thy grace, to
confess my sins, to do penance, and to amend my life. Amen.

What Should We Confess?

We now understand what Confession is, and why it is important to voice our sins to a priest who is acting in persona Christi. But what exactly should we confess?

Consider the path to holiness as a swim toward grace. If you tried to swim with bulky clothes on, you would have a rather difficult time. In fact, if you tried to swim with a thick coat and heavy shoes, you might even drown. Mortal sins are such as these: cumbersome clothing items which get in the way of reaching the tranquil ponds of grace. Such items must be shed for us to swim freely and effectively.

Now let's consider another aspect of this swim effort. It might surprise some folks to learn that very holy persons such as Pope John Paul II and Mother Teresa frequented the sacrament of Reconciliation daily! How could this be?

It would be helpful to think of such individuals as holy Olympians. An Olympic swim athlete covers his head with a smooth cap and shaves his entire body so that not even a tiny hair will hold him back from achieving his fastest race time ever. Each sin could be thought of like one of these small hairs attached to the flesh. Individually, they are hardly noticeable and do not make much of a difference. But all together, they provide a significant amount of drag to the soul that is striving to finish the good race and reach sanctification.

If bulky clothing is like mortal sins, then small hairs would be like venial sins. Mortal sins sever us from God's grace and therefore endanger us in losing our souls. Venial sins damage but do not sever our relationship with God.

Put another way, venial sins hinder our souls from

enjoying optimal spiritual health; mortal sins deteriorate our souls like a spiritual disease.

Fortunately, God's grace is abundant. We must seek reconciliation with him. Jesus instituted Penance for each member of the church, as we are all sinners in need of God's mercy. Penance is "above all for those who, since Baptism, have fallen into grave sin, and have thus lost their baptismal grace and wounded ecclesial communion. It is to them that the sacrament of Penance offers a new possibility to convert and to recover the grace of justification" (CCC 1446).

What Do the Saints Say?

ST. ISIDORE OF SEVILLE expressed the profound hope held within this merciful sacrament.

Confession heals, confession justifies, confession grants pardon of sin, all hope consists in confession. Through confession, there is a chance for mercy.

We are graciously offered a new dawn, a new day, another chance, which must not be wasted.

Reflection

What attachments hinder us in our journey toward optimal spiritual health?

Time For Prayer

Repentance Prayer

Dear God,

I come to you as a sinner who is undeserving of your grace and presence.

I repent all my sins and ask you to forgive me so that my request may be heard by you.

Lord, have mercy on me and fill me with your grace.
Wash me with the blood of your son, Jesus Christ, that I may shine and walk unashamed.

I ask for your favor from this moment to the end of the day. I thank you, for you are faithful.

Amen.

How Reconciliation Brings Us Closer to Christ and the Church

The Christian religion centers around a relationship with God. The sacrament of reconciliation offers the primary work of renewing that relationship. This act in which we humble ourselves, admit our wrongs, and sincerely promise to do better "consists in restoring us to God's grace and joining us with him in an intimate friendship." For the penitent who enters the confessional with a contrite heart, reconciliation is often followed by "peace and serenity of conscience with strong spiritual consolation" (CCC 1468). Such an amendment of the relationship between child and Father restores the life of grace to the Christian.

Reconciliation also repairs the relationships with each other which were broken by sin. "The forgiven penitent...is reconciled with himself...with his brethren...with the Church. He is reconciled with all creation" (CCC 1469). Simply put, once a person restores peace in his soul, the divisions he experiences within himself and with others are corrected. Peace in the world must begin in the heart of each individual.

What Do the Saints Say?

ST. BRIDGET OF SWEDEN received several revelations from God in the 14th century. She wrote extensively about the sorrows of Christ, admonishing the faithful to cease sin and bring consolation to the Lord. She encouraged regular confession as a means to strengthen the soul.

Just as an animal becomes a stronger beast of burden and more beautiful to behold the more often and better it is fed, so too confession—the more often it is used and the more carefully it is made as to both lesser and greater sins—conveys the soul increasingly forward and is so pleasing to God that it leads the soul to God's very heart.

Thus, the sacrament of confession not only increases the sinner's spiritual health but also directs the Christian closer to the source of its strength—Christ himself.

Reflection

How does the grace of having a good relationship with Christ flow improve our relationships with others?

Time For Prayer
Hail, Holy Queen

Hail, holy Queen, Mother of mercy, our life, our sweetness and our hope.

To thee do we cry, poor banished children of Eve.

To thee to we send up our sighs, mourning and weeping in this valley of tears.

Turn, then, most gracious advocate, thine eyes of mercy toward us; and after this, our exile, show unto us the blessed fruit of thy womb, Jesus.

O clement, O loving, O sweet Virgin Mary:

V. Pray for us, O holy Mother of God,

R. That we may be made worthy of the promises of Christ.

Let us pray.

O God, whose only-begotten Son, by His life, death and resurrection, has purchased for us the rewards of eternal life, grant, we beseech Thee, that meditating on these mysteries of the most holy Rosary of the Blessed Virgin Mary, we may imitate what they contain, and obtain what they promise, through the same Christ our Lord.

Amen.

3 PRAYER

- *What Is Prayer?*
- *When Should We Pray?*
- *What Are Different Types of Prayer?*
- *How Did the Lord Teach Us to Pray?*
- *Formal and Informal Prayer*

When we think of prayer, we might think of a child kneeling at her bedside, hands folded, head down, asking for God to watch over her while she sleeps. Or we might think of a monk in a church, fasting and pleading for the end of a plague that is devastating the community. Prayer is both of these things. Yet, just as human communications vary in form and purpose, from the informal phone call to a speech presentation, prayer also takes on many forms. It should not be relinquished as something belonging only to innocent children or pious monks. Prayer is for everyone.

What Is Prayer?

In the most basic sense, it is a conversation with God. A person can be taking a walk through the woods and voicing their thoughts and concerns and directing these sentiments to God as if He were walking beside them. This would be a basic prayer.

In its most intense moments, intercessory prayer can be exhausting. Scripture tells us that in the Garden of Gethsemane, Jesus knelt "in agony [as] He was praying very fervently; and His sweat became like drops of blood" (Luke 22:44).

The Church tells us that "prayer is the raising of one's mind and heart to God" (CCC 2559). We, the creatures, recognize and pay homage to the Creator. The first step in offering a prayer is to acknowledge that there is a power higher than oneself. Humility develops when we understand that the power to foresee or control all outcomes is not within our human power. Only God is all-knowing and all-powerful. This realization allows us to enter into prayer— communication with God.

What Do the Saints Say?

ST. FAUSTINA OF POLAND confirms that every soul, whether cold, fervent, or tepid, has a reason to practice prayer.

A soul arms itself by prayer for all kinds of combat. In whatever state the soul may be, it ought to pray. A soul which is pure and beautiful must pray, or else it will lose its beauty; a soul which is striving after this purity must pray, or else it will never attain it; a soul which is newly converted must pray, or else it will fall again; a sinful soul, plunged in sins, must pray so that it might rise again. There is no soul which is not bound to pray, for every single grace comes to the soul through prayer.

Every soul needs grace; therefore, every soul requires prayer as the medium through which to gain grace.

Reflection

If I were to win a ten-minute phone call with God, what would I tell him?

Time For Prayer

Catholic Morning Prayer

O Jesus, through the Immaculate Heart of Mary, I offer you my prayers, works, joys, and sufferings of this day for all the intentions of you Sacred Heart, in union with the holy sacrifice of the Mass throughout the world, in thanksgiving for your favors, in reparation for my sins, for the intentions of all my associates, and especially for the intentions of our Holy Father, the Pope.
Amen.

When Should We Pray?

If prayer is a conversation with God, when should we pray? Many times, people fall into an "emergencies only" policy when turning to prayer, such as, "Dear God, please help me ace this interview." Certainly, such a plea for help contains an acknowledgment of God's supremacy over the path of our lives. However, we must not resort to treating the Good Lord as a heavenly vending machine, such that we put in a token prayer and expect to receive the benefit of a refreshment.

As God's children, we are designed to relate to the Heavenly Father on a much more intimate level. Jesus' sacrifice on the cross opened the gates of heaven for us. Afterward, the Holy Spirit descended to strengthen and sanctify the faithful. From the moment of Pentecost, God's Law was written on our hearts. Therefore, "In the New Covenant, prayer is the living relationship of the children of God with their Father who is good beyond measure, with his Son Jesus Christ and with the Holy Spirit" (CCC 2565). In prayer, we address each person of the Holy Trinity at once.

When a person approaches a good friend, they do not communicate only to ask for a favor. If they did, the friendship would quickly dissolve. Between friends, the communication comprises of compliments, apologies, appreciation, and requests. Such communication is desirable for an effective prayer life as well.

What Do the Saints Say?

ST. THERESE OF LISIEUX, who often wished to think of herself as God's Little Flower, humbly spoke of prayer in the simplest terms.

Prayer is an aspiration of the heart, it is a simple glance

directed to heaven, it is a cry of gratitude and love in the midst of trials as well as joy; finally, it is something great, supernatural, which expands my soul and unites me to Jesus.

It is a glance, a remembrance of the One who never for a moment ceases to remember us in his loving-kindness.

Reflection

What are three blessings I have experienced over the past week for which I would like to give thanks; what are three concerns I have which I would like to entrust to the Lord?

Time For Prayer
Closing Prayer for Divine Mercy Chaplet (optional)

Eternal God, in whom mercy is endless and the treasury of compassion inexhaustible, look kindly upon us and increase Your mercy in us, that in difficult moments we might not despair nor become despondent, but with great confidence submit ourselves to Your holy will, which is Love and Mercy itself.

What Are Different Types of Prayer?

When we prepare ourselves to pray, it is helpful to remember the ACTS: Adoration, Contrition, Thanksgiving, and Supplication.

Adoration is an acknowledgment of God's magnificence and is rightly given to him alone. The Magi and the shepherds, upon learning of the birth of Christ, journeyed to Bethlehem, saying, "We have seen [the king's] star in the east, and are come to adore him" (Matthew 2:2).

Contrition is a recognition that God calls each of us to holiness and that we regularly fall short of fulfilling that call. The apostle Peter, upon hearing the cock crow the morning after Jesus' abduction, repented of having three times denied knowing Jesus; "he broke down and wept" (Mark 14:72). When Peter offered the Lord a contrite heart, Jesus forgave him.

Thanksgiving stems from an awareness that none of us is entitled to God's grace. It flows to us through the goodness of God and should therefore be received with gratitude. Mary Magdalen poured fragrant "expensive ointment...and anointed the feet of Jesus and wiped his feet with her hair" to show her profound gratitude for his mercy in forgiving her for her transgressions (John 12:3).

Supplication is a petition for God's blessing. We trust that he knows all things, and desires good things for us as a father wishes good for his children. We ask for God's aid in our trials. The woman in the crowd, in a great act of trust, reached out to Jesus "and touched the edge of his cloak, and immediately [she was healed]" (Luke 8:44).

What Do the Saints Say?

ST. EPHRAEM OF SYRIA stressed that prayer provides the channel through which graces flow and virtues are formed.

Virtues are formed by prayer. Prayer preserves temperance. Prayer suppresses anger. Prayer prevents emotions of pride and envy. Prayer draws in the soul of the Holy Spirit and raises man to Heaven.

Prayer lifts our hearts to God and leads us along a more righteous life path.

Reflection

What virtue would you like the Lord to mentor you into developing?

Time For Prayer

Come, Holy Spirit

Come Holy Spirit, fill the hearts of your faithful and kindle in them the fire of your love. Send forth your Spirit and they shall be created. And You shall renew the face of the earth.

O, God, who by the light of the Holy Spirit, did instruct the hearts of the faithful, grant that by the same Holy Spirit we may be truly wise and ever enjoy His consolations, Through Christ Our Lord.   Amen.

How Did the Lord Teach Us to Pray?

Often, people are confused about how to pray. Even the apostles asked Jesus, "Lord, teach us to pray" (Luke 11:1). Jesus offered them the fundamental Christian prayer, called the Lord's Prayer or the Our Father. This prayer, given to the apostles by the Lord himself, is the most excellent of all prayers. It contains all the basic elements of what a good prayer should contain. The Lord's Prayer begins with an acknowledgement of who God is, followed by seven petitions.

We begin by recognizing that we are part of God's family, and rightly address him as "Our Father who art in Heaven." We remember that God is the perfect father, residing in heaven and that we hope to be united with him after this life has passed. We speak to God with childlike love, trust, and respect. We speak of ourselves in the collective sense because none of us is isolated in faith. Together, we act as the Body of Christ.

The petitions which follow reflect the nature of God and our proper relationship with him. We begin with "Hallowed by Thy name" recalling the second commandment to honor God's name by speaking it reverently. Next, we petition, "Thy Kingdom come" remembering that our most ardent desire should be that God's kingdom of divine grace and love might be established in our hearts and throughout the world. The third petition asks, "Thy will be done on earth as it is in Heaven"; in this way, we submit ourselves always to

God's holy will, trusting that the Father desires what is best for us.

The later petitions grow more specific in interest. We ask that the Lord "give us this day our daily bread," seeking sustenance for our body and soul. We are reminded to receive God's blessings with gratitude, knowing that he will provide for all we need. The fifth petition contains a condition and is one of the most challenging: "Forgive us our trespasses, as we forgive those that trespass against us." In this petition, we plead for God's mercy upon us, yet we are also called to be merciful to others.

Knowing that we strive to live a good life, pleasing to God, we ask that the Lord "lead us not into temptation." And if we must follow the Lord into adversity, as soldiers would follow their beloved general, we plead that God would give us sufficient grace to overcome the enemy and thus finish victorious. Only through the practice of resisting and conquering vice may we root ourselves in virtue. Wrestling with temptation indeed tests our morals and leads us to strengthen our character, however, we humbly ask in the final petition that the Lord "deliver us from evil." We recognize the cunning and danger of evil and wish to preserve ourselves from eternal damnation.

What Do the Saints Say?

ST. ALPHONSUS LIGUORI OF NAPLES offered consolation during times of struggle.

It often happens that we pray God to deliver us from some dangerous temptation, and yet God does not hear us but permits the temptation to continue troubling us. In such a case, let us understand that God permits even this for our greater good. When a soul in temptation recommends itself to God, and by His aid resists, O how it then advances in perfection.

Much as a precious metal is refined by fire, our souls are made virtuous by struggles.

Reflection

Which petition of the Lord's Prayer speaks most directly to your heart? What is it about this petition that catches your attention?

Time For Prayer

The Lord's Prayer

Our Father, Who art in heaven, hallowed be Thy name.

Thy Kingdom come. Thy will be done on earth, as it is in heaven.

Give us this day our daily bread. And forgive us our trespasses as we forgive those who trespass against us.

And lead us not into temptation but deliver us from evil. Amen.

Formal and Informal Prayer

As mentioned before, prayer is for everyone. Prayer is also for every occasion. There is persevering prayer, which arises from the deepest intentions of our hearts. This might be a plea for God to resolve an impending and dire situation. Or it may be something more long-term, such as a beloved one's conversion. When we pray with fortitude and trust, submitting our desires to God's holy will, we are encouraged by Christ's words: "Ask and it will be given to you; seek and you will find; knock and the door will be opened to you" (Matthew 7:7).

Yet, sometimes, we have no words for the desires of our hearts. Sometimes, we can do no more than sit with God and gaze at him in his Holy Presence. This is acceptable as well. This is what we know as meditative prayer—prayer in its simplest form. This basic practice of prayer is becoming increasingly difficult in modern times, as it requires an effort to clear the mind from distractions and simply focus God's love and mercy.

Think of a loving couple who learns all about each other until an exchange of words is no longer needed. They simply gaze at each other and smile. So it is with Jesus and us as the Church, his bride. In response, he returns our gaze with mutual affection.

In another sense, think of a mother with her newborn infant. The babe has no words to communicate his love for her and even if he tries, it comes out as babbles and gurgles. And yet, the mother delights in every little coo the infant utters. Still, it is enough that he looks upon her face with wonder. So it is with the Heavenly Father and us as his children. In turn, the Father's loving presence and intent gaze fill us with security and wellbeing.

The Rosary is one of the most beautiful forms of meditative prayer. In the Rosary, we meditate on the life of Christ and ask the Blessed Virgin Mary to pray for us. The Rosary is a gospel prayer since its words are taken directly from the first books of the New Testament of the Bible. The Hail Mary is from the book of Luke, when the angel, Gabriel, greets the Virgin Mary. The majority of the mysteries of the Rosary are taken directly from scripture. For example, the First Joyful Mystery is the Annunciation, when the angel, Gabriel, informs Mary that she has been chosen to be the mother of our Savior, Jesus Christ, who is God. The Third Joyful Mystery prompts us to meditate on the Nativity of Our Lord, the birth of Christ. The Fifth Sorrowful Mystery reminds us of Christ's great love for us as He died on the cross so that we could receive His grace. The First Glorious Mystery is about the Resurrection of Our Lord, a glorious event indeed. These are all events taken straight from the Bible.

What Do the Saints Say?

ST. IGNATIUS OF LOYOLA emphasized the fraternal nature of prayer, encouraging us to reveal our hearts to the Lord.

We must speak to God as a friend speaks to his friend, servant to his master; asking some favor, acknowledging our faults, and communicating to Him all that concerns us, our thoughts, our fears, our projects, our desires, and in all things seeking His counsel.

We approach God as a friend and confidant, trusting that he will mentor us well on our journey toward holiness.

Reflection

How can we create a space and set aside a time for meditation?

Time For Prayer
Hail Mary

Hail Mary, Full of Grace, the Lord is with you.

Blessed are you among women, and blessed is the fruit of your womb, Jesus.

Holy Mary, Mother of God, pray for us sinners now, and at the hour of our death.

Amen.

4 CHARITABLE LOVE

- *What Does Christ Teach Us about How to Love?*
- *How Are We to Love God?*
- *How Are We to Love Our Neighbor?*

When we consider love in a Christian context, we often recall John 3:16, the frequently quoted scripture which tells us, "For God so loved the world that he gave his one and only Son, that whoever believes in him shall not perish but have eternal life." How does this verse express Christian love? It contains key elements which help us understand the true nature of love: a desire for another's good, the sacrifice of one's own contentment and comfort, and action-oriented toward the long-term goal of salvation.

What Does Christ Teach Us about How to Love?

Cardinal Levada's glossary defines charity (love) as, "the theological virtue by which we love God above all things for his own sake, and our neighbor as ourselves for the love of God." Therefore, we love the Holy Trinity God because He is our Creator, our Savior, our Sanctifier.

Our love goes beyond a feeling of gratitude due to the

gifts He gives us, such as life and peace. Also, our love for God is deeper than what He does for us, such as ease a difficult situation or enable someone to be well disposed to our requests. All in all, we love God for who He is, not just for what He does for us.

When asked which of the commandments given to Moses was the most important, Jesus answered: "The first is, 'Hear, O Israel: The Lord our God, the Lord is one; and you shall love the Lord your God with all your heart, and with all your soul, and with all your mind, and with all your strength. The second is this, 'You shall love your neighbor as yourself.' There is no other commandment greater than these" (CCC 2196).

Notice how Jesus answers the question of the greatest commandment with a two-part answer. Evidently, the two are intertwined. We cannot love God and ignore our neighbor, but we must love God first in order to properly love our neighbor.

Jesus illustrates this concept as the vine and the branches. The Lord is the vine, the source, the stronghold for us who act as the branches, reaching out into the world. Jesus assures us that "If you keep my commandments, you will abide in my love, just as I have kept my Father's commandments and abide in his love" (John 15:10). Therefore, love is not only trust but obedience. Every parent experiences this when raising a child. The parental love is abundant and unconditional; however, the child greatly pleases the parent when following the parent's loving guidance.

50

Jesus implores us to stay rooted in His love "[so] that my joy may be in you, and that your joy may be full" (John 15:11). When we are filled with God's love and have joyful hearts, only then are we effective in spreading God's light and love to others. Only then can we bring others to Him for salvation.

God is love—benevolent, sacrificial, holy charitable love. As 1 John 4:19 states: "We love because he first loved us." We can love others properly only when rooted in the One who is love.

What Do the Saints Say?

ST. POPE JOHN PAUL II OF POLAND supported the necessity of allowing God's will to firmly instruct our own.

Take away from love the fullness of self-surrender, the completeness of personal commitment, and what remains will be a total denial and negation of it.

We must submit ourselves to God's direction and commit ourselves to seek His guidance as part of our daily bread. The sacrifice is necessary but sweet.

Reflection

What hesitations do we have in surrendering our will to God's? How can we recognize that God is on our side and move beyond these hindrances?

Time For Prayer

Teach Us To Love

Lord, we thank Thee for all the love that has been given to us, for the love of family and friends, and above all for Your love poured out upon us every moment of our lives in steadfast glory.

Forgive our unworthiness. Forgive the many times we have disappointed those who love us, have failed them, wearied them, saddened them.

Failing them we have failed You and hurting them we have wounded our Savior who for love's sake died for us. Lord, have mercy on us, and forgive.

You do not fail those who love you. You do not change nor vary. Teach us Your own constancy in love, Your humility, selflessness and generosity.

Look in pity on our small and tarnished loving, protect, foster and strengthen it, that it may be less unworthy to be offered to You and to Your children.

O Light of the World, teach us how to love.
Amen.

How Are We to Love God?

Jesus taught us that the best way to love God is to trust in His holy will and submit ourselves to him, even when it is difficult. We witness the greatest example of this during Jesus' agony in the garden as He faced the upcoming persecution, way of the cross, and crucifixion. Praying in the darkness of that Holy Thursday night, Jesus foresaw the fullness of the sacrifice which would be required of Him for the salvation of souls. In his humanity, he trembled with fear and sweat drops as of blood, pleading, "Father, if you are willing, take this cup pass from me." Still, Jesus summoned His strength to make a bold act of submission, continuing the prayer with, "yet not my will, but yours be done" (Luke 22:42).

Jesus offers the parable of the Prodigal Son in the Gospel of Luke 15:11–32 to illustrate how God's children can sometimes stray or outrightly reject God. We sometimes fall into childish ways, desiring affection without the duty of fulfilling our responsibility or the requirement of submitting to authority. The Father's love will not diminish. However, a healthy spirituality requires commitment on our part. The Father loves us with longing and mercy, even when we turn our backs on Him.

This story tells of a son who brazenly asked for his father's inheritance while his father still lived, then squandered it on worldly pleasures until he was poor and in a desperate state. Figuring that his father's servants are better off than he was, the son returned to his father's house to beg for a job. He did not dare hope for forgiveness nor mercy but believed that he might at least get some food and shelter.

The father sees the son from a long way off and rejoices upon his return. Jesus describes the scene:

He ran to his son, embraced him and kissed him. His son said to him, "Father, I have sinned against heaven and against you; I no longer deserve to be called your son." But his father ordered his servants, "Quickly bring the finest robe and put it on him; put a ring on his finger and sandals on his feet. Take the fattened calf and slaughter it. Then let us celebrate with a feast because this son of mine was dead, and has come to life again; he was lost and has been found." Then the celebration began.

The father not only took the son back into his household; he prepared a feast to celebrate his son returning to his senses.

So it is with our heavenly Father when we turn back to Him. He does not hold it against us but embraces us and rejoices upon our return.

What Do the Saints Say?

ST. CLARE OF ASSISI confirms that we become most like the object of our desires.

We become what we love and who we love shapes what we become. If we love things, we become a thing. If we love nothing, we become nothing. Imitation is not a literal mimicking of Christ, rather it means becoming the image of the beloved, an image disclosed through transformation. This means we are to become vessels of God's compassionate love for others.

For this reason, we are encouraged to think of those things which are true, beautiful, and holy.

Reflection

What do you spend most of your time thinking about? How can you infuse more thoughts of what is true and holy into your day?

Time For Prayer

Recommendation to the Sacred Heart of Jesus

O Sweetest Heart of Jesus, to Thee I commend my body and my soul this night, that they may calmly rest in Thee. And as I cannot praise my God while I sleep, do Thou deign to supply my lack of service, and for every beating of my heart give praise to the most Holy Trinity on my behalf; receive into Thyself every breath I draw and offer them all to God as glowing sparks of Divine love.
Amen.

How Are We to Love Our Neighbor?

In Romans 13:8-10, The apostle Paul reminds us of the greatest commandments as given to Moses: "He who loves his neighbor has fulfilled the law. The commandments, 'You shall not commit adultery, You shall not kill, You shall not steal, You shall not covet,' and any other commandment, are summed up in this sentence, 'You shall love your neighbor as yourself.' Love does no wrong to a neighbor; therefore, love is the fulfilling of the law" (CCC 2196).

Indeed, the first three of the ten commandments are oriented toward the love of God while the remaining seven commandments are oriented toward neighbor. Worded positively and simply, they can be listed as follows:

1. Love God above all.
2. Love God's name.
3. Observe God's day.
4. Honor your father and mother and those who care for you.
5. Respect each person's life and reputation.
6. Respect the vows of marriage.
7. Generously give of your goods and talents.
8. Speak kindly and truthfully about others.
9. Nurture your own relationships.
10. Care for your own goods as blessings.

Ultimately, to be a follower of Christ is to live by the Golden Rule as Jesus commanded: "Do unto others as you would have them do unto you" (Luke 6:31).

Our Lord illustrated this in practical terms through the parable of the Good Samaritan, found in the Gospel of Luke

10:30-37. As the story goes, when a man was traveling, "He fell among robbers, who stripped him and beat him, and departed, leaving him half dead." Three persons came across the man and each reacted according to what he thought was best. The priest passed the victim by on the other side, not wanting to taint himself, lest the man is dead. Likewise, a Levite (one of the chosen people of God) saw the beaten man and passed by on the other side.

However, a Samaritan—a person not expected to do good by others—came across the half-dead man "and when he saw him, he had compassion, and went to him and bound up his wounds, pouring on oil and wine; then he set him on his own beast and brought him to an inn, and took care of him. And the next day he took out two denarii and gave them to the innkeeper, saying, 'Take care of him; and whatever more you spend, I will repay you when I come back.'"

Jesus recalls the original question regarding who is our neighbor, by asking, "Which of these three, do you think, proved neighbor to the man who fell among the robbers?" And when the man listening to the parable responded that the one who acted neighborly was the one who showed mercy, Jesus instructed him, "Go and do likewise."

And so the Lord commands us all to go and do likewise. No matter who we are or who the other person is, we are to treat each person as if we were the gentle hands and feet of Christ. We are to treat each person as if they were Christ in need.

What Do the Saints Say?

ST. In Romans 13:8-10, The apostle Paul reminds us of the greatest commandments as given to Moses: "He who loves his neighbor has fulfilled the law. The commandments, 'You shall not commit adultery, You shall not kill, You shall not steal, You shall not covet,' and any other commandment, are summed up in this sentence, 'You shall love your neighbor as yourself.' Love does no wrong to a neighbor; therefore, love is the fulfilling of the law" (CCC 2196).

Reflection

Recall a time when someone did a small act with great love; compare this with a time when you experienced a similar act with very little love. How can you mindfully practice small acts with great love?

Time For Prayer
A Prayer for Kindness in All Things

Dear Lord,

I praise You as the essence of all things loving. You are complete in Yourself. You are unconditional in Love.

In my heart I desire to be more like You, and I invite You to be with me as I move about through my day. When I begin to compare myself to others, let me remember that we are all made in Your likeness, and that each of our bodies is a temple of Your Holy Spirit.

When I am tempted to make judgments about the actions, behaviors, or even the looks of others as a way of making myself feel better, come to my aid and bring about in me a spirit of contentment, a spirit of gratitude.

Help me to treat each person I encounter as I would like to be treated and fill me with loving kindness so that my thoughts, words, and deeds flow from Your Spirit of unconditional Love.

Let me remember You always. Let me be ever aware of Your presence in each moment of my life, as I would surely cease to live, to move, to have my being if thought of me falls from Your mind's embrace for the span of even one breath; for it is Your breath that gives me life.

I ask all these things through Christ who strengthens me.

Amen.

5 CHRISTIAN SERVICE

- *How Were We Created?*
- *Are All Men Created Equal?*
- *How Are We Designed to Need One Another?*
- *How Are We Called to Serve One Another?*

The natural consequence of genuine love is service. Christians serve others because we love God. Thus, when we look upon our neighbor, we view him as a Christ in need. When we serve our neighbor, we do so as a Christ in service.

How Were We Created?

Jesus told His disciples, "the Son of Man did not come to be served, but to serve, and to give his life as a ransom for many" (Mark 10:45). If God became incarnate to serve others, then service must be essential to our purpose as disciples of Christ.

Through the story of Creation, we retrace our roots to one set of parents: Adam and Eve. We learn in Genesis 1:27 that "God created man in His own image; in the image of God He created him; male and female He created them."

Thus, we all belong to the same family, descending from

the original man and woman God created. How privileged we are to have a mind, and a body, and a soul to reflect God's love for us and to respond in returning God's love to Him.

God created each of us in His own image. Yet, individuals can represent only a small facet of who God is. If we consider ourselves each as a gem facet, we must allow the jeweler to cut and polish us so that we can clearly shine God's light to the world.

The shining glory is not our own. Instead, we strive to be transparent, ridding ourselves of the cloudiness caused by sin so that Christ's light may shine more fully through us. We work collectively to bring forth light. The divine light shines even more brilliantly as each soul submits himself to the jeweler's work.

The great theologian Aquinas argues in his Summa Theologica that "Diversity comes about by the intention of God to communicate His goodness to creatures and to represent His goodness though them. As any one creature is finite and therefore cannot provide an adequate representation of God's goodness, God produces diverse creatures so that the inadequacy of the representation of anyone may be made up by others" (Question 47, A1). Therefore, our diversity works together to express various aspects of God's goodness.

God created us as male and female, though not as two half-images. Rather, humans are made to be complementary. We were designed to need one another. And it is only when the complementary persons join together—in a complete offering of self to one another—that

61

our love results in a life-giving miracle, creating another human being.

What Do the Saints Say?

ST. AUGUSTINE OF HIPPO explained how we can recognize the embodiment of genuine love.

What does love look like? It has the hands to help others. It has the feet to hasten to the poor and needy. It has eyes to see misery and want. It has the ears to hear the sighs and sorrows of men. That is what love looks like.

Much the way Christ pointed to His works when asked if he was the Messiah, we should be able to point to our service when asked if we have truly loved our neighbor.

Reflection

How can we better serve those in need in our own family, in our own community?

Time For Prayer

Prayer For A Spirit of Service

Dear loving Lord, You sent Your Son to serve. You sent Him to give His life for me. Let Your Spirit awaken in me the same spirit of service. Let me not look for position or gain. Instead, show me how to let others go before me. Make me meek, make me humble so I too can give my life—willfully, obediently, and faithfully—even when it hurts, in love, with Christ, and like Christ. In Jesus' name.

Amen.

Are All Men Created Equal?

Our human equality results from two areas. Firstly, we are "equally endowed with rational souls...." We each "have the same nature and the same origin." Secondly, each individual is "redeemed by the sacrifice of Christ" and therefore we are each called to holiness. Therefore, due to our common heritage in creation and redemption, we all "enjoy an equal dignity" (CCC 1934).

Mankind's equality refers to each man's dignity and rights. It does not refer to personal amounts of talents, resources, or privileges. We all have equal dignity as God's children, and equal rights to pursue a path to holiness.

According to Aquinas, "inequality exists in creation for the benefit of the whole and must be attributed to God's wisdom in the same way as diversity is accounted to God" (Question 47, A2). The whole of Creation is ordered in a hierarchy, from the celestial seraphim to the dutiful army ant. To accept one's position in the world is to live with humble gratitude.

In this way, the holy saints can do much to inspire us. Royals and house servants, missionaries and cloistered, virgins and mothers, theologians and mystics have all found a path to sainthood; we can too. All are called to serve others in their own capacity and to assist one another toward Heaven.

For this reason, as Christians, we strive to view each other as brothers and sisters in Christ, regardless of physical distinctions or social class differences. A good Christian king has a great responsibility before God to protect his many subjects, encourage then toward virtue, and ensure that authorities do their jobs well.

A good Christian house servant has a much narrower scope of responsibility, yet he is still called to complete his duties to the best of his abilities and answer the call to holiness in his own station of life.

Both are called to serve God with a humble heart. Both are called to serve others with love and kindness. Both must patiently bear the crosses that come with their given positions. The king may not go wherever he pleases whenever he desires, as he is expected to be an upstanding example of virtue to the citizens and must be accessible to the people who need him. Likewise, the house servant may not make a show of himself and speak however he pleases, lest he bring dishonor and scandal to the master of the house.

What Do the Saints Say?

ST. LOUIS TEZZA OF ITALY affirmed that holiness is for all persons in every state of life.

God's invitation to become saints is for all, not just a few. Sanctity therefore must be accessible to all. In what does it consist? In a lot of activity? No. In doing extraordinary things? No, this could not be for everybody and at all times. Therefore, sanctity consists in doing good, and in doing this good in whatever condition and place God has placed us. Nothing more, nothing outside of this.

Sanctity derives from good works which flow from a devout faith in God.

Reflection

What qualities in others do you consider when determining a person's holiness? How can you improve these qualities in yourself?

Time For Prayer

Prayer To Lovingly Serve Others

God our Father, Yours is the beauty of creation and the good things you have given us.

Help us to begin this day joyfully in Your name and to spend it in loving service of You and our fellow man.

We ask this through our Lord Jesus Christ, Your Son, who lives and reigns with You and the Holy Spirit, one God, for ever and ever.

Amen.

How Are We Designed to Need One Another?

None of us is equipped with everything necessary to thrive physically and spiritually. Men are created to need one another. What small infant can survive even one week without another person to nourish him, hold him, and bathe him? Likewise, what child can teach himself the faith? Even Jesus came in the form of an infant dependent on Mary and Joseph's loving care and instruction. How much more so must we need the assistance and wisdom of others for our own physical and spiritual needs?

The Church recognizes that differences in humanity are present, dependent on "age, physical abilities, intellectual or moral aptitudes, the benefits derived from social commerce, and the distribution of wealth. The 'talents' are not distributed equally" (CCC 1936). Certainly, there are wise elders and wonderous toddlers, athletes and intellectuals, beggar saints and humble philanthropists—all who help each other thrive.

None of these 'talents' excludes the others. Some wonderful people enjoy vibrancy, athleticism, astute intellect, and piety. These people are the great gems of humankind, yet even they would quickly praise those who helped them along. Pope John Paul the Great was one such man—vivacious, agile, creative, and faithful—yet he often attributed his priestly success to his father's pious example of praying on his knees in the early morning.

Recognizing our own need for others inspires us to give to those in need us since Jesus tells us, "As you did it to one of the least of these my brethren, you did it to me" (Matthew 25:40). Christ's New Law challenges us to love not only our neighbor but also our enemies.

To truly love, however, is to desire holiness for each person's soul. Therefore, we avoid permitting others to sin on the pretense of loving them. Rather, we call others to holiness because we genuinely desire for them what is good and true. Thus, we are to love the sinner, but not the sin. To truly love the sinner is to offer the mercy that Jesus gave to Mary Magdalen, saying, "Go and sin no more" (John 8:11).

What Do the Saints Say?

ST. ST. JOHN OF DAMASCUS points to the host of heavenly saints as the best persons to mentor us through this life.

The saints must be honored as friends of Christ and children and heirs of God. Let us carefully observe the manner of life of all the apostles, martyrs, ascetics, and just men who announced the coming of the Lord. And let us emulate their faith, charity, hope, zeal, life, patience under suffering, and perseverance unto death so that we may also share their crowns of glory.

There are saints for persons of each temperament and every station in life. It is good for us to study their example for guidance and inspiration.

Reflection

What saint most inspires you in your current season of life?

Time For Prayer

Prayer To Serve God With Love

Lord, help us to follow the example of saints who have gone before so that we may serve You with love and obtain perfect joy.

We ask this through our Lord Jesus Christ, who lives and reigns with you and the Holy Spirit, one God, forever and ever.

Amen.

How Are We Called to Serve One Another?

Understanding that God created us to need one another, and that service should flow from love, how exactly are we to serve one another? The works of mercy tell us how. There are corporal works of mercy oriented toward the body and spiritual works or mercy oriented toward the soul.

Let us look first at the corporal works of mercy, as you cannot satisfy a man's soul before offering him bread to satisfy his body.

Corporal Works of Mercy

1. Feeding the hungry.
2. Giving drink to the thirsty.
3. Clothing the naked.
4. Sheltering the homeless.
5. Visiting the sick.
6. Visiting the imprisoned (or ransoming the captive).
7. Burying the dead.

Satisfy hunger and thirst by serving at a soup kitchen. Also, avoid hoarding or wasting food and water.

Clothe the naked by donating gently used clothes or new socks to shelters. Provide shelter by donating blankets or medicines.

Visiting the sick and imprisoned can include calling an elderly neighbor, offering a frozen meal to a postpartum family adjusting to a newborn, or a donation to the local blood bank, or an anonymous letter encouraging an inmate.

Burying the dead shows respect for a good life lived. We pray for the soul of the deceased and remember that we are all on a journey aspiring for heaven and we hope for the Resurrection.

Once a person begins charitable giving, he or she often realizes that there is so much more they would like to contribute than their daily duties allow. Therefore, seek a good charity that works toward the change you desire to support. Set up a monthly donation to that nonprofit giving homeless teens a meal and a safe bed for the night. Join the mailing list of a crisis pregnancy center working with women desperately seeking a way to keep their babies. Find an organization doing work that you are passionate about and give what you can.

Spiritual Works of Mercy give the necessary boost for moving forward in a healthy way.

Spiritual Works of Mercy

1. Counseling the doubtful.
2. Instructing the ignorant.
3. Admonishing the sinner.
4. Comforting the sorrowful.
5. Forgiving injuries.
6. Bearing wrongs patiently.
7. Praying for the living and the dead.

Counseling the doubtful offers hope in Christ's promise of salvation. We are told in 1 Corinthians 1:25 that "the foolishness of God is wiser than human wisdom, and the weakness of God is stronger than human strength." When someone is struggling to bear their cross, encourage them that Christ is the Way, the Truth, and the Life. Share a good spiritual book that offers clarity and comfort. Invite the person to accompany you to an upcoming prayer meeting or Sunday Mass.

Good Catholic catechism is a treasure to be shared. Learn

your faith through good reading, podcasts, videos, classes, and conferences. When you set out to instruct or even correct others, do so as Christ did, in patience and love. Admonishing the sinner is simply helping others find their way back to God. Humbly acknowledging that we are all sinners, we mercifully correct others when they stray from the heavenward path. Offer some good resources explaining the truth and beauty of God's ways. Pray with your friend for strength to live in virtue.

Bearing sorrows alone puts people at terrible risk of despair. When we see that someone is suffering, we can reach out through a card, a phone call, or a home-cooked meal. Small acts of kindness do much to soothe the soul.

Forgiving injuries is most challenging, especially when we're still hurting. Write a letter expressing your suffering and what will enable you to let go of your grievance. Even if you never send it, writing it out will provide clarity and release. Pray the Divine Mercy Chaplet in reparation for offenses throughout the world.

Firmly placing our hope in the Lord makes it easier to bear wrong patiently. Unite your sufferings with Christ, and trust that the truth will eventually come to light.

Praying for those who have gone before us and those who are with us still helps us recall that we are all God's children seeking to enjoy eternal life with the heavenly Father. Request a Mass to be offered for a deceased loved one. Pray a rosary for a struggling friend. Collect a "spiritual bouquet" of sacrifices and prayers for a suffering family. The graces will be strongly felt and greatly appreciated as a tremendous blessing.

What Do the Saints Say?

ST. PHILIP NERI OF ROME speaks of the challenge in forgiving offenses.

If a man finds it very hard to forgive injuries, let him look at a Crucifix, and think that Christ shed all His Blood for him, and not only forgave His enemies, but even prayed His Heavenly Father to forgive them also.

Let us emulate Christ in forgiving others, even while the offense still stings.

Reflection

What hurts do I need to bring to Christ on the cross? For what offenses do I need to ask forgiveness?

Time For Prayer

A Prayer For The Grace to Forgive

Dear Lord,

I come to You with a heart that is heavy with resentment. The hurt I carry with me is taking its toll, slowly closing the door of my heart to love.

I have been unjustly hurt and I don't want to forgive, yet, I beg you to grant me the grace to forgive the one who has hurt me, even though the very thought of doing so is painful to me.

Turn my eyes now to You and show me Your wounds. Show me Your bloody face. Show me Your torn flesh.

Help me to always remember that You are the True Victim who was suffered the most unjust hurt ever known to humankind.

Give me the grace to be sorrowful for my sins that nailed You to the cross and whisper in my ear Your loving words, "Father forgive them for they know not what they do." With Your tenderness, O Lord, I know my heart will melt and be filled with Your love, that I may forgive my offender. Amen.

6 EVANGELIZATION

- *What Does It Mean to Evangelize?*
- *Why Should Sharing the Faith Matter?*
- *Why Is Conversion Necessary for All Souls?*

Many Catholics get the feeling that evangelization simply isn't exactly Catholic. The Church carries the stories of the great missionary saints such as Isaac Jogues, Junipero Serra, and Francis Xavier. Yet, the work of converting other people to the faith seems to be a relic of the past. Worse yet, it is deemed to be a work that only other faiths undertake, such as Mormons or Jehovah's Witnesses. We must learn to speak to others about the Good News of the Lord in a way that coincides with our rich Catholic identity.

What Does It Mean to Evangelize?

Evangelization means bringing the Good News of the Lord into everyday situations and pointing others to the path which leads to true knowledge of God and genuine happiness. If we seek to follow the call to love our neighbor, then this is what we should naturally desire for each person we encounter.

Winning over souls for Jesus is not about keeping a

scorecard that we can present to St. Peter when we get to the gates of heaven. It is about living a life that provides a clear signpost guiding others in a positive direction. Proclaiming the Gospel will require more than simple living, however. We will be called upon to share our knowledge of the One True Faith and defend it when necessary. Pope Paul VI in Evangelii Nuntiandi (On Evangelization in the Modern World) stated, "There is no true evangelization if the name, the teaching, the life, the promises, the Kingdom and the mystery of Jesus of Nazareth, the Son of God are not proclaimed."

Evangelization implies different things depending on our current relationship with Christ. For those living and practicing the Catholic faith, evangelization is a call to ongoing growth and renewed conversion. For those who have accepted the faith in name only, it is a call to re-evangelization. For those who have ceased practicing their faith, it is a call to reconciliation and renewal in the faith life.

For children learning the faith and not yet confirmed, evangelization is a call to formation toward discipleship through the family faith and religious education. For our separated Christian brethren, it is an invitation to the fullness of faith found in the one, holy, catholic, and apostolic Church. For those not claiming any faith, evangelization is a call to conversion to know Jesus as Christ and thus experience a new life with Christ in the Church.

EVANGELIZATION for ALL

✦ Practicing Catholic > renewed conversion

✦ Nominal Catholic > re-evangelization

✦ Fallen Away Catholic > reconciliation and renewal

✦ Catholic students > formation toward discipleship

✦ Non-Catholic Christians > invitation to fullness of faith

✦ Non-Christians > call to conversion to begin a new life in Christ

True faith transforms hearts. Transformation shows growth. Growth exhibits life. Without personal transformation on a continuous basis, faith is dead. As long as faith is alive, it works to transform us to be more Christlike.

What Do the Saints Say?

ST. PHILARET DROSDOV OF MOSCOW speaks of how living faith is one willing to counter the culture for the sake of holiness.

A fish that is alive swims against the flow of water. One that is dead floats down with the water. A true Christian goes against the current of a sinful age. A false one is swept away by its swiftness.

Christianity requires vigilance against a swift down current.

Reflection

In what aspects do I find myself carried about by the current culture? How can I strengthen myself to combat negative influence?

Time For Prayer

Prayer For Courage

Lord, give me courage in my everyday life. Courage to speak Your truth and to defend the faith. Courage to follow Your commandments and to live Your beatitudes.

Courage to live a moral life, even if it means losing friends. Courage to pray. Courage to love others, especially the poor. Courage to visit the sick and the lonely.

Lord, may I not fall back in fear, but may I do Your will, strengthened by Your love.

Why Should Sharing the Faith Matter?

Ongoing conversion is our daily responsibility. Some persons experience a gradual conversion over the course of many years. While others are inspired through ordinary family relationships and friendships. Still, others experience conversion through retreats, parish missions, or other specific spiritual encounters provided by various spiritual movements in the Church.

The emphasis is on catching the flame of the Holy Spirit in our hearts. Once lit, it is important to preserve the fire of renewed spiritual interest so that it does not quickly extinguish. Only a lit candle can provide a flame to light another. Or as Christ explained in Matthew 5:13, "But if salt loses its taste, with what can it be seasoned?"

As Christians, we profess the life, death, and resurrection of Jesus. We proclaim God as eternally faithful who creates all in love and sustains all with His gracious care. We humbly accept God's unconditional love and His offer of divine life, even despite our sins, failures, and faults. This offer is available not only to us but to all mankind. Yet, God needs us to be His instruments in proclaiming the Good News.

When we respond to God in faith and repentance, we join with His Body, the Church. We become His people. We are empowered with new life in the Holy Spirit and guided to our eternal life with the heavenly Father.

In the Christian view, the universe and all that is in it have been created to share God's life. To follow Jesus means that we choose right for ourselves and share God's life with others. Out life's purpose is not an endless quest for power and riches. Rather, it is an ongoing formation in knowing, loving, and serving God and neighbor. We do this by offering to the Lord the little we have in the hopes that He will bless our humble offerings with His almighty power. For "with God, all things are possible" (Matthew 19:26). We must trust in God's promise, "Behold, I make all things new" (Revelation 21:5).

Salvation history includes the story of countless individual souls but also of peoples: the Israelites, the Greeks, the Franks, the Normans. The Gospel is the good news for all of society, with its values, laws, and systems. The Word of God transforms individuals as well as the entirety of human existence. Therefore, individuals are called to shine forth their Christian lights to transform communities, organizations, and society in general.

Justice and peace, fairness and holiness—these are the marks of a civilized society. These are the fruits of evangelization. Our manner of service to one another shows the depths of our acceptance of the Gospel. To maintain one's faith as merely a personal spirituality or to worship a personal version of Jesus is not fulfilling Christ's call to proclaim the Good News.

What Do the Saints Say?

ST. IGNATIUS OF ANTIOCH emphasizes the necessity for authenticity when evangelizing.

It is better to keep silent and be something than to talk and be nothing. Teaching is an excellent thing, provided the speaker practices what he teaches. Now, there is one Teacher who spoke, and it was done. But even what He did silently is worthy of the Father. He who has made the words of Jesus really his own is able also to hear His silence. Thus, he will be perfect: he will act through his speech and be understood through his silence. Nothing is hidden from the

Lord; no, even our secrets reach Him. Let us, then, do all things in the conviction that He dwells in us. Thus, we shall be His temples and He will be our God within us. And this is the truth, and it will be made manifest before our eyes. Let us, then, love Him as He deserves. Directing people properly in the faith requires living genuinely in the faith.

Just as actions speak louder than words, sometimes pensive silence speaks more clearly than words said insincerely.

Reflection

What areas of my life could be improved to be more authentic to my walk as a Christian?

Time For Prayer

Prayer For The New Evangelization

Heavenly Father, pour forth Your Holy Spirit to inspire me with these words from Holy Scripture.

Stir in my soul the desire to renew my faith and deepen my relationship with your Son, our Lord Jesus Christ, so that I might truly believe in and live the Good News.

Open my heart to hear the Gospel and grant me the confidence to proclaim the Good News to others.

Pour out your Spirit, so that I might be strengthened to go forth and witness to the Gospel in my everyday life through my words and actions.

In moments of hesitation, remind me:

- If not me, then who will proclaim the Gospel?
- If not now, then when will the Gospel be proclaimed?
- If not the truth of the Gospel, then what shall I proclaim?

God, our Father, I pray that through the Holy Spirit I might hear the call of the New Evangelization to deepen my faith, grow in confidence to proclaim the Gospel and boldly witness to the saving grace of Your Son, Jesus Christ, who lives and reigns with You, in the unity of the Holy Spirit, one God, forever and ever.

Amen.

Why Is Conversion Necessary for All Souls?

Evangelization is directed both to ourselves and to others. It points both inward and outward. For ourselves, it beckons us to continually receive the Gospel of Jesus Christ, promoting our conversion as individuals and ultimately as Church. Outwardly, evangelization addresses those who are unaware of the Gospel teachings or those who have heard them but have rejected them.

In Redemptoris Missio, Pope John Paul II's encyclical on missionary activity, he stated three objectives for proclaiming the Good News:

1. to proclaim the Gospel to all people

2. to help bring about the reconversion of those who have received the Gospel but have not taken it to heart

3. to deepen the Gospel in the lives of believers.

We may not be missionaries in foreign lands or officially pagan territories. However, we are called to proclaim the Good News wherever we are. We can do this through maintaining a positive attitude in the workplace, offering a word of hope to a discouraged friend, or explaining Church teaching to a relative who struggles with knowing how to vote on current issues.

It is important to remember that life is more than a journey involving checking off bucket list items. Those once-in-a-lifetime experiences are exciting, but they do not make up who we are. Ultimately, the one and only item that should surpass all is: LIVED A LIFE WORTHY OF AN ETERNITY IN HEAVEN—(check).

When we keep this in mind, it makes sense to assess our daily choices by the question: Did my choices this day move me a little closer to heaven? Through evaluating ourselves regularly, we work on continual conversion. In evangelizing to others, we assist them in attaining the end goal of heaven as well.

What Do the Saints Say?

ST. FRANCIS XAVIER OF SPAIN cautioned the faithful

to be gentle with those seeking a fresh start.

Take care not to frighten away by stern rigor poor sinners who are trying to lay bare the shocking state of their souls. Speak to them of the great mercy of God and make easy for them what is at best a difficult task. Tell them that whatever they have to say will be no news to you. Sometimes people are helped by your telling of your own lamentable past.

We are to remember that we are all sinners in need of God's gracious mercy.

Reflection

How can we better encourage others to seek the path toward heaven?

Time For Prayer

Eternal God (By St. Francis Xavier S.J.)

Eternal God, Creator of all things, remember that You alone created the souls of unbelievers, which You have made according to Your image and likeness.

Behold, O Lord, how to Your dishonor, many of them are falling into Hell.

Remember, O Lord, Your Son Jesus Christ, who so generously shed His Blood and suffered for them.

Do not permit that Your Son, Our Lord, remain unknown by unbelievers, but, with the help of Your Saints and the Church, the Bride of Your Son, remember Your mercy.

Forget their idolatry and infidelity, and make them know Him, whom You have sent, Jesus Christ, Your Son, Our Lord, who is our salvation, our life and our resurrection, through whom we have been saved and redeemed, and to whom is due glory forever.

Amen.

7 PURPOSE

- *What Is God's Purpose for Our Lives?*
- *God's Promise of Purpose*
- *How Do We Explore This Purpose?*
- *How Can We Be Sure We Are on the Right Path?*

There comes a time in each of our lives when we feel the smallness of our being compared to the rest of the world. It might be during a trip to the beach when we stand at the edge of the breaking waves and stare into the expanse of the ocean. It might be after a hike up a mountain summit when we look upon the vast view showing us more of the world than we've ever seen before. Or it might be in the midst of a crisp evening as we gaze into the darkening sky and witness pinpoints of light shining forth their majestic glow.

We sense that we are but a speck in the mighty expanse of the universe and that our life is but one breath of an eternal Creator. In such profound humility, we wonder, What is my purpose?

What Is God's Purpose for Our Lives?

God continuously draws His people to himself and therefore it is natural for us to seek Him. "The desire for God is written in the human heart, because man is created by God and for God; and God never ceases to draw man to

85

himself. Only in God will he find the truth and happiness he never stops searching for..." (CCC 27).

The St. Joseph Baltimore Catechism answers the question about purpose in the most basic sense: God made me to know Him, to love Him, and to serve Him in this world, and to be happy with Him forever in heaven (Question 6).

When it comes to realizing God's intended purpose for your life, there are three basic phases of discovery:

1. Desiring to have a purpose.
2. Searching for what that purpose may be.
3. Embracing your purpose once you discover it.

Looking at this in a literal sense, the word desire comes from two root words, de and sire, the meaning of the father. Thus, true desire flows from the Father.

This is why the only path to true happiness is found in God. Our Creator placed this compass within us so that we might be able to navigate through the deep waters of life. As Psalm 37:4 instructs, "Take delight in the Lord, and He will give you the desires of your heart."

According to CCC 293, "Scripture and Tradition never cease to teach and celebrate this fundamental truth: 'The world was made for the glory of God.'" Therefore, when we use our God-given talents to give glory to the Almighty, we are likewise rewarding ourselves by fulfilling our purpose.

The catechism continues, citing St. Bonaventure's explanation that "God created all things 'not to increase his glory, but to show it forth and to communicate it', for God has no other reason for creating than his love and goodness: 'Creatures came into existence when the key of love opened his hand.'"

What Do the Saints Say?

ST. LOUIS DE MONTFORT encouraged confidence in prayer, trusting in God's benevolence.

Pray with great confidence, with confidence based upon the goodness and infinite generosity of God and upon the promises of Jesus Christ. God is a spring of living water that flows unceasingly into the hearts of those who pray.

When we turn to prayer, God pours into us His own spirit, revitalizing us to continue the journey ahead.

Reflection

What aspects of God do we appreciate most? How can we approach God with greater confidence in His benevolence?

Time For Prayer
Prayer For Vision and Instruction

Dear God,

We pray that You would remind us that that we are all a part of building and expanding Your Kingdom.

We ask that you give us a fresh vision for Your purpose for our lives.

We ask that You open our eyes, our ears, our hearts, and our minds to your vision so that we can live out our purpose. Remove anything from our lives that hinder us from discerning Your vision.

We pray that You would draw us closer to You as you bring us revelation to our purpose. Please reveal to us what we need to do today to not run wild, but rather be focused on Your divine vision.

In Jesus' Name, Amen.

God's Promise of Purpose

Our purpose, and God's glory, "consists in the realization of this manifestation and communication of his goodness, for which the world was created." When we order our lives toward glorifying God, we are able to enjoy the peace of knowing that we are becoming who we are created to be; we finally feel at home. God made us 'to be his [children] through Jesus Christ, according to the purpose of his will...' for 'the glory of God is man fully alive...'" (CCC 294).

The unfolding of one's particular purpose in life often comes in the quiet, reflective moments, sometimes especially after a time of adversity. As the Bible says, God's voice is heard not in the earthquake or the fire, but in stillness (1 Kings 19:11-13).

We can begin with absolute confidence that God created each of us with a purpose in mind. For no creator sets out to create things aimlessly. God's abundance of love overflows into His creative works. And we know that this purpose for which we are created is good, as God is good.

Jeremiah 29:11-14 reveals: "'For I know the plans I have for you,' declares the Lord, 'plans to prosper you and not to harm you, plans to give you hope and a future.'" The declaration is evident, and additionally, it attaches to it a hope of interest and exploration.

The passage continues, "'Then you will call on me and come and pray to me, and I will listen to you. You will seek me and find me when you seek me with all your heart. I will be found by you,' declares the Lord, 'and will bring you back....'" Thus, the Lord desires that we seek Him wholeheartedly with sincere love. And when we do so, He will eagerly respond.

The five divine promises contained in this passage anchor us in hope:

1. God has a plan for each of us—plans for our welfare, not for woe.
2. God's plans will provide a future filled with hope.
3. God will listen to us when we call upon Him.
4. God will allow Himself to be found when we wholeheartedly seek Him.
5. The Lord will draw us near to Himself and set us

once again on the path toward heaven.

What Do the Saints Say?

ST. MARGARET MARY ALACOQUE OF FRANCE emphasized the peace that comes with detachment.

But above all preserve peace of heart. This is more valuable than any treasure. To preserve it there is nothing more useful than renouncing your own will and substituting for it the will of the divine heart. In this way, his will can carry out for us whatever contributes to his glory, and we will be happy to be his subjects and to trust entirely in him.

Our happiness stems from giving glory to God.

Reflection

What attachments can you identify which distract you from maintaining peace? How can you challenge yourself to release these things a little at a time?

Time For Prayer

Prayer To Be The Genuine Article

Dear God,

I want to be the genuine article. I don't want to be watered down. Diluted.

I want Your strong and pure love to come through me in a genuine way. Genuine love coming through me in a way that will bless others. With a divine sincerity—nothing fake.

I pray to become a better person by allowing love to freely flow through me without restriction. Without alteration. As genuine as You are, dear God.

Amen.

How Do We Explore This Purpose?

To be able to find, we first must seek. How do we know when an answer is given?

Sometimes circumstances can steer us in a multitude of directions. What our parents, our siblings, or our friends expect from us may not coincide with our God-given purpose. Turbulent situations such as job loss, an unexpected illness, or the death of a loved one can lead us into desperation where our only focus is to bail water and stay afloat. Yet even such stormy situations can lead us to discover our life's work when we refuse fear and embrace faith.

The Holy Spirit bestowed upon each of us certain spiritual gifts to strengthen God's Kingdom. While God does not will any evil to happen to us, He can bring good out of any circumstance. It may be through that we find our purpose during a particularly trying time in life. Perhaps we experience a painful tragedy such as losing a child in a drunk-driving accident. Then we discover that our purpose is to organize groups to prevent such accidents from happening to other families.

During the canonization homily for Jesuit Peter Faber, Pope Francis boldly declared that "An authentic faith always implies a deep desire to change the world... and our desires expand our hearts." Even if our mission is not one of leadership, we can still bless those around us in small ways through a gentle smile, a word of encouragement, a small gift picked especially for someone needing consolation. Through making a gift of ourselves and doing acts of kindness from the heart, we will find that work that satisfies our spirit—the purpose for which God created us.

What Do the Saints Say?

ST. CATHERINE OF SIENNA spoke of God's creative love for all the world.

We are such value to God that he came to live among us ... and to guide us home. He will go to any length to seek us, even to being lifted high upon the cross to draw us back to himself. We can only respond by loving God for his love.

How do we respond with adequate love? Catherine instructed: Be who God meant you to be and you will set the world on fire.

Reflection

What small step can we take toward becoming a better version of ourselves?

Time For Prayer

<u>*Prayer To Find the Right Path*</u> *(by Thomas Merton)*

My Lord God, I have no idea where I am going. I do not see the road ahead of me. I cannot know for certain where it will end. Nor do I really know myself, and the fact that I think I am following Your will does not mean that I am actually doing so.

But I believe that the desire to please You does in fact please You. And I hope I have that desire in all that I am doing. I hope that I will never do anything apart from that desire. And I know that if I do this You will lead me by the right road, though I may know nothing about it.

Therefore, I will trust You always though I may seem to be lost and in the shadow of death. I will not fear, for You are ever with me, and You will never leave me to face my perils alone.

How Can We Be Sure We Are on the Right Path?

Oftentimes, we may feel like passengers on a ship navigating through a vast expanse of ocean with no land in sight. We may check our compass and study the heavens but unless we have an idea of the general direction in which we should be heading, we will soon become lost at sea!

We seek the heart of the Creator and invite Him into our lives to direct us. Indeed, we step aside, allowing Him to take the helm of our life's ship and navigate us through the treacherous seas.

Remember that God's heart is benevolent, and He does not create us for a purpose that will leave us miserable. On the contrary, we achieve personal fulfillment when we embrace our life's purpose. Just as a working dog is eager to pull a load and a bird is at ease in flight, our spirit is driven to fulfill our purpose; it soars once that purpose is found.

To know what is true of God, we must appeal to our reason but also follow our hearts. Our hearts provide the compass by which we navigate through the waters of life. As temples of the Holy Spirit, we offer prayer from our hearts. Therefore, we must seek our God-given purpose by connecting to God through prayer. Essentially, "According to Scripture, it is the heart that prays. If our heart is far from God, the words of prayer are in vain" (CCC 2562).

This is where practicing daily devotions and frequenting the sacraments can be especially helpful. Through such practices, we acquire grace and clarity to know God's will for our lives.

To say that I know something in my heart is to say that I understand it with the essence of my being. Likewise, "The heart is the dwelling-place where I am, where I live...the heart is the place 'to which I withdraw.' The heart is our hidden center...only the Spirit of God can fathom the human heart and know it fully." Most importantly, "The heart is the place of decision..." (CCC 2653).

The heart is the source from which most sacred decisions are made. Jesus warns that "The thief comes only to steal and kill and destroy; I came that they may have life and have it abundantly" (John 10:10). When seeking the things of God, we must understand the aspects of God's nature:

⊗ God is Truth.
⊗ God is Light.
⊗ God is Life.
⊗ God is Love.

When we think we have found our purpose, we must put it to the test. Does this work lead us to be a more authentic version of ourselves? Do our family, friends, and acquaintances notice that we seem to walk a little lighter? Do we feel more creative when working in this capacity? Are we more oriented to loving God, ourselves, and others when dedicating ourselves to this vocation? If the answer is yes to all four of these, then you have found a fitting purpose.

What Do the Saints Say?

ST. MARY MACKILLOP OF AUSTRALIA implored the faithful to entrust all cares to the Holy Family.

Have courage, trust in God, St Joseph and our Blessed Mother, and you need have no fear...Trust in God's Providence, interfering—as it always does—for our own good.

We can depend on God's Providence; it does exactly as the name entails, providing for our every need.

Reflection

Recall a time when God answered your prayer with a solution you could not have considered yourself. What path can you presently entrust to the Lord for guidance?

Time For Prayer

Prayer for Confidence in the Revealed Purpose

Dear God,

Thank You that even if what we see in front of us doesn't feel good or look good, Your plans are good. That even if harm comes our way, you'll use it for good.

Thank You for the hope we can find in You. We trust that You have our future planned out from the very beginning. Allow us to rest in You and rest in Your master plan.

Give us the confidence that You have nothing but good planned for us. Remind us that even though we don't know the full plan, that You know the plan. May we lean into You. In Jesus' Name, Amen.

8 THE CHURCH

- *A Return to Proper Order and Communion*
- *Holy Mother Church*
- *The Rock of Our Foundation*
- *What Are the Functions of the Church?*

When we discuss the Church of God, we refer to the faithful, along with the magisterium in union with the pope. The Church is comprised of the persons who act as Christ's hands and feet, Christ's eyes and ears, Christ's comforting arms and encouraging words.

The beauty of Christ's Church is that God, through His Holy Spirit, acts through His baptized children who willingly submit themselves to be instruments of His work on earth. As Mother Teresa of Calcutta expressed, "I am a pencil in the hand of God." The beauty of God's Holy Church is reflected by the degree to which her faithful submit to God's holy will.

A Return to Proper Order and Communion

To look at the origins of the Church, we must go all the way back to the beginning, with the creation of Adam and Eve: the original parents of mankind, the first family, the first Domestic Church. Those first Church members, through their willful disobedience, severed their solid relationship with the Lord. Thus, sin dispersed mankind in its very origins.

Sin broke the union and communion bonding God and man. Our destiny was to live in intimate communion with the Creator of all things and to enjoy life in Him. However, the beautiful story turned tragic when sin entered the scene. God's children were scattered—the first family was permanently wounded. The proper order of relationships between God and mankind and between man and woman went askew.

God the Father greatly desired a restoration of the relationship between Himself and mankind. Therefore, He sent His only Son, the Spotless Lamb, to redeem what had been lost. Through this sacrifice, the Father beckoned for His children to return to Him.

This calling for mankind to return to proper order and communion with God, is described in the Catechism thusly: "The gathering together of the Church is, as it were, God's reaction to the chaos provoked by sin" (CCC 761).

What Do the Saints Say?

ST. BONIFACE OF ENGLAND noted that the Church's course is best set straight by those who stay aboard.

The Church is like a great ship being pounded by the waves of life's different stresses. Our duty is not to abandon ship, but to keep her on her course.

As the Church faithful, we all share the duty to care for the baroque of Peter.

Reflection

What kept you aboard during the times when you were tempted to abandon ship in regard to the Church? How can you use that experience to encourage others?

Time For Prayer

Pentecost Prayer

O Holy Spirit, divine Spirit of light and love, I consecrate to You my understanding, my heart, my will, my whole being for time and for eternity.

May my understanding always be submissive to Your heavenly inspirations and to the teachings of the Holy Catholic Church, of which You are the infallible Guide.

May my heart ever be inflamed with love of God and of my neighbor.

May my will always conform to the divine will, and may my whole life be a faithful imitation of the life and virtues of our Lord and Savior Jesus Christ, to whom be honor and glory forever.

Amen.

Holy Mother Church

If God is calling us to return to Him, why is it necessary that we do so in unison? Why can't we just sit in our homes and pray our own private prayers of thanksgiving, repentance, and worship?

We, humans, hunger for purpose in our lives. We intuitively sense that we each have been created for a mission beyond mere existence. The Catholic Church states that God made us to know, love, and serve Him in this world, so we can be with Him forever in heaven.

Yet, the Catholic Church would not point us to our mission without equipping us with the tools we need to journey toward fulfilling that call. The Church offers Scripture, her magisterial teachings, the Tradition of the sacraments, sacramentals, the examples of all the saints, and the church community itself to encourage and support us along the way.

We are all flawed and prone to making daily excuses for our weaknesses. We continually need God's forgiveness and healing in order to start anew. The Catholic Church offers this new beginning through the Sacrament of Reconciliation. This sacrament is offered to us as many times as we need it, so we should participate in it often.

Any parent understands that a child left on his own may be able to care for himself for a brief amount of time. Depending on his age and capabilities, a youth might last a few hours or even a few days on his own. Perhaps the child is able to make himself a sandwich for lunch, but he leaves out all the food items to spoil. Perhaps he puts his dirty dishes in the dishwasher but does not use the correct dish soap in the machine, resulting in a pool of bubbles spreading through the kitchen. Perhaps he even uses a towel to soak up the mess but neglects to place the towel in the clothes washer.

While the child's efforts are sincere and admirable, eventually, the youth will require a parent's assistance and guidance on how to do better next time. The same is true for our relationship with Holy Mother Church. We can get by for a time on our own, but eventually, we will need the guidance and teachings of the Church to steer us back on the correct path.

What Do the Saints Say?

ST. POPE PIUS IX emphasized the maternal nature of the Church founded by Christ.

There is only one true and holy religion, founded and instituted by Christ Our Lord. Mother and Nurse of the virtues, Destroyer of vice, Liberator of souls, Guide to true happiness, she is called Catholic, Apostolic, and Roman.

Like a holy mother, the Church nurtures, protects, liberates, and guides us to holiness.

Reflection

How can we abide in Christ by participating more fully in

the life of the Church?

Time For Prayer
Prayer For the Church #3

O God! our refuge and our strength, look down with favor on Thy people who cry to Thee; and through the intercession of the glorious and Immaculate Virgin Mary, Mother of God, of Saint Joseph her Spouse, of Thy blessed Apostles Peter and Paul, and of all the Saints, in mercy and goodness hear our prayers for the conversion of sinners, and for the liberty and exaltation of our holy Mother the Church. Through the same Christ our Lord.

Amen.

The Rock of Our Foundation

Just as our families must be built on a firm foundation of faith, we must live in a community with others to be able to grow in our faith. The Church provides a community of faith-filled friends offering support and strength in our journey.

Only in the Catholic Church do we experience the fullness of the seven sacraments. These are the rituals that Christ Himself instituted so that we might gain grace and draw closer to the Lord. Through the Catholic Church, we are privileged to enter into intimate communion with Christ through the sacrament of the Eucharist—His own body and blood offered for us. He longs to feed us with Himself and we long to partake of this Divine sustenance. This integral relationship is illustrated in John 15:5 which states: "I am the vine; you are the branches. Whoever abides in me and I in him, he it is that bears much fruit, for apart from me you can do nothing."

Finally, participating in Church community is necessary due to the Catholicism being the one true faith. The Catholic Church is the one Church established by Christ Himself (Matt 16:18). It is the universal Church, embracing all peoples and fully equipping them on the journey toward holiness.

What Do the Saints Say?

ST. POPE PAUL VI OF ITALY explains in Lumen Gentium, section 7 the formation of the mystical Body of Christ.

In human nature united to Himself the Son of God...redeemed man and re-molded him into a new creation. By communicating His Spirit, Christ made His brothers, called together from all nations, mystically the components of His own Body. In that Body the life of Christ is poured into the believers who, through the sacraments, are united in a hidden and real way to Christ who suffered and was glorified.

United with other Catholic Christians, we are reformed as individuals and transformed into a sacred whole.

Reflection

How can we better utilize the tools the Church offers us the tools for transforming us into a new creation?

Time For Prayer

Prayer For A New Creation

Jesus, thank you for not wanting to just fix our lives but make of us a 'new creation.'

Holy Spirit, we ask You to show us the beauty of the life You have planned for us.

We give You this time together and ask for the grace to share openly and allow our hearts and minds to be transformed by Your love.

Amen.

What Are the Functions of the Church?

The collective Church is described in several terms. It is the Temple of the Holy Spirit, the Bride of Christ, and the Body of Christ. Let us explore these different terminologies and their meaning.

When Christ founded His Church, he addressed Simon the Apostle, giving him a new name, saying: "...you are Peter, and upon this rock, I will build my church, and the gates of the netherworld shall not prevail against it" (Matthew 16:

18). With these words, Jesus made it clear that the Church—singular and unified—is under His authority. For this reason, official dogmatic Church teaching is noted to be infallible.

Naturally, this infallibility doctrine does not apply to the persons comprising the Church body. If it did, there would not be centuries of history laced with heretics and schisms.

To further examine the teaching of infallibility, we are called to appreciate it as a gift preserving Christ's Church from error in teachings. The Catechism of the Catholic Church states: "It is this Magisterium's task to preserve God's people from deviations and defections and to guarantee them the objective possibility of professing the true faith without error.... To fulfill this service, Christ endowed the Church's shepherds with the charism of infallibility in matters of faith and morals" (CCC, 890).

Truth cannot contradict itself. In this way, the Church acts as the Temple of the Holy Spirit.

The prophets of the Old Testament prepared for Christ as the Bridegroom of the Church. This relationship was affirmed by John the Baptist who spoke of the Church as a bride "betrothed" to Christ so as to become one spirit with Him. Christ gave Himself for this unblemished bride so that He might sanctify her.

Christ "has joined her with himself in an everlasting covenant and never stops caring for her as for his own body" (CCC, 796). Much as Christ is the spotless Lamb, the Church is the spotless Bride of Christ.

The integral nature of the relationship between the Church and Christ is so profound that it is also referred to as His Mystical Body. This Body is noted by People Pius XI as the "universal Sacrament for the salvation of mankind" (Lumen Gentium, 48). Much as Christ offers us His own flesh and blood in the Eucharist to sustain us, Christ offers His Mystical Body—the Church—to keep the Spirit within us alive.

Much as a coal cannot stay ablaze when removed from the coalbed, individuals need community to stoke the fervency of their faith and keep it aflame.

Jesus established the Church as a means for our salvation. The Church is like the toolbox offering the means for sanctification. Apart from her, we will struggle mightily to efficiently attain holiness. That is not to say it is impossible, but the task can be completed much more quickly and effectively with the proper tools and a supportive community. We reflect Christ on earth to the degree that all the members of Christ's Body concern themselves with the will and the work of the Lord.

The Church is the extension of the Divine Incarnation; the Word became flesh and dwelt among us (John 1:14). When the God-Man, Jesus, ascended to heaven, he poured forth His Divine Spirit upon the apostles—the first members of His Church—so that the work of the Lord might carry on. For this reason, the Church is called the Body of Christ.

What Do the Saints Say?

ST. POPE LEO I OF ROME professed the purity of the Church as Christ's holy spouse:

The Church is a virgin, the bride of one Spouse, Who is Christ, and this Church does not allow herself to be violated by any error; so that, throughout the whole world there may be for us one incorruptness of a single chaste communion.

As protector and fortifier, Christ maintains that His Bride's teaching authority is inviolable.

Reflection

Which function of the Church—Temple of the Holy Spirit, Bride of Christ, Body of Christ—speaks to me most clearly?

Time For Prayer

A Prayer for Devoted Laity in the Church

O Lord, our God, You called Your people to be Your Church. As they gather together in Your Name, may they love, honor, and follow Your Son to eternal life in the Kingdom He promised.

Let their worship always be sincere and help them to find Your saving Love in the Church and its Sacraments.

Fill with the Spirit of Christ those whom You call to live in the midst of the world and its concern. Help them by their work on earth to build up Your eternal Kingdom. May they be effective witnesses to the Truth of the Gospel and make Your Church a living presence amid the world.

Increase the gifts You have given Your Church that Your faithful people may continue to grow in holiness and imitation of Your Beloved Son.

9 HOLINESS

- *What Great Works Must I Do to Be a Saint?*
- *Is Sanctity Always Serious?*
- *How Can I Find Joy in Suffering?*

To describe someone as saintly summons an image of a docile, prayerful soul, donning a golden halo and an unblemished tunic, palms pressed together, eyes lifted toward heaven. The difficulty with such an image being our icon of sainthood is that we rarely ever see such a sight in real life, and therefore we become convinced that there are no living saints among us. The reality can often be quite different. Mother Teresa frequently pressed her palms against her face when seeking God's grace to walk amid the slums of India for one more day. Pope John Paul II practiced the habit of kissing the ground before preaching to the crowds in a new country. Both of these modern figures were known to be bold, joyful—and holy.

What Great Works Must I Do to Be a Saint?

Mother Teresa lived as a simple nun working among the poor, opening homes for orphans and the dying. Meanwhile, Pope John Paul II held the highest office in the Church, writing numerous encyclicals, meeting with officials from countries throughout the world and instructing the faithful in how to live for God amidst troublesome modern times.

These two figures were recognized in their time as living saints. Yet who among us will ever have the opportunity, much less the virtue, to hold the hand of even one dying stranger? Who among us will ever be asked to write a catechetical guide to instruct the faithful of even one church parish? What can we do to live holy lives and progress along the path toward sainthood?

The question from Matthew 19:16 comes to mind: "Teacher, what good thing must I do to obtain eternal life?"

The good news is that there have been numerous saints throughout history. There are living saints even today all throughout the world. While most of these holy men and women will be recognized and beloved by those who knew them, they may not achieve the popularity and the documented miracles necessary to be officially canonized by the Church.

What many people do not realize is that the saints were able to do great things because they first established had a habit of doing little things well. Jesus responded that the necessary key to eternal life was in keeping the commandments. Look first to the Mosaic commandments when seeking sanctity. Are we centering our lives around God, giving Him due respect and primacy in our daily actions? Are we generous with our neighbors, taking care of the needy in our families and our communities?

Do we approach our daily duties as blessings rather than burdens? Do we do the job to the best of our ability with a loving desire to please our Lord? If we are given a task such as cleaning out the car for a spouse, do we remove all the junk and meticulously vacuum the crevices so that we can present the clean vehicle as a pleasant surprise? Or do we instead toss out an empty water bottle and a crumpled napkin but leave the floor full of crumbs so we can shrug our shoulders and mutter that at least we tried?

When we cultivate spiritual practices which help us respond to the promptings of the Holy Spirit, that is when we grow in virtue. When we meet our daily trials with virtue, it becomes easier to overcome dire situations with heroic sanctity.

These daily acts of virtue must stem from a love of God. When we focus on the face of Jesus—not the turbulent waters surrounding us—we are able to move easily, lightly, miraculously toward our Beloved Savior.

What Do the Saints Say?

ST. GEORGE MATULAITIS-MATULEWICZ OF VILNIUS, who renovated the Congregation of Marian Fathers of the Immaculate Conception, wrote of our innate desire for perfection.

We must perfect ourselves in the spiritual life by choosing those spiritual exercises which especially impel us toward conscious spiritual living...[and] we must try to help others achieve holiness, for by serving others, by contributing to their greater holiness, we grow holy and soar higher ourselves.

Thus, seeking holiness for ourselves and others is a win-win situation, aiding all along the proper path toward our ultimate end goal—heaven.

Reflection

What difficult accomplishments have I been able to achieve because love pushed me through the challenges? How can I apply that same motivation to my spiritual life?

Time For Prayer

Prayer For Holiness

Breathe in me,
O Holy Spirit,
that my thoughts may all be holy.

Act in me,
O Holy Spirit,
that my work, too, may be holy.

Draw my heart,
O Holy Spirit,
that I love only what is holy.

Strengthen me,
O Holy Spirit,
to defend all that is holy.

Guard me so,
O Holy Spirit,
that I may always be holy.

Amen.

Is Sanctity Always Serious?

Many of us maintain the idea that holiness involves perpetually dwelling on the world's dire circumstances. We think that we should preoccupy ourselves with the woes of the world and the multitude of crises present all around. We recall the opening line in the Act of Contrition: Oh my God, I am heartily sorry for my sins because I dread the loss of heaven and the pains of hell.

In fact, the opposite is true for those seeking holiness. We do not set our eyes on the troubles of fallen humanity. Rather, we gaze lovingly on the face of Jesus. When we spend time getting to know Him—His purpose, His sacrifice, His plan and desire for us—then we can grow in holiness and move the world to be a better place. It is then that we remember the second line in the Act of Contrition: [I am heartily sorry] most of all because [my sins] offend You, my God, who are all good and deserving of all my love.

Therefore, to ask if sanctity is always serious is akin to asking, Is love always serious? Love is certainly a serious matter, but the draw of love is its exuberant joy, not its sobriety. Love carries a mystical ability to transform each of us into the best version of ourselves. So also does sanctity.

Viewing love from a parental outlook, the very moment a child emerges into the world, the parents rejoice and delight in every little movement, every smirk and grimace, the newborn makes. They also shudder at every potential harm, diligently cleaning all the baby clothes, washing their hands before picking him up, checking every food label, toy, and device that will come in contact with the newborn to ensure the safety of their precious loved one.

We would be wise to take as many precautions for the salvation of our souls and the souls of our loved ones. Such diligence stems only from the proper attitude, however. We do this not because we fear that God will wag a stern finger at us otherwise. Rather, we can do this because we love God and our neighbor with such depth that we cannot imagine this life—or the afterlife—without Him!

Sanctity begins with love. Each morning and evening and frequently throughout the day, take note of God's little signs of love for you: the sun gently shining, a songbird sweetly twittering, a new bud softly blooming in the garden. Then respond with small acts of love for God: spending ten minutes in spiritual reading and prayer, diligently setting out all the breakfast items so the kids can get breakfast easily, subtly placing the keys by the wallet to ensure your spouse's timely departure for work. Each of these acts could be done to avoid trouble and other people's anger, but they are much better accomplished through a spirit of love.

What Do the Saints Say?

ST. JOSÉMARIA ESCRIVÁ OF SPAIN, promoter of the lay vocation emphasized that the love that leads to sanctity is a love that pervades every action:

Do you really want to be a saint? Carry out the little duty of each moment; do what you ought and put yourself into what you are doing. Persevere in the exact fulfillment of the obligations of the moment. That work—humble, monotonous, small—is prayer expressed in action, which prepares you to receive the grace of that other work—great and broad and deep—of which you dream. Didn't you see the light in Jesus' eyes when the poor widow left her little alms in the Temple? Give Him what you can; the merit is not in whether it is big or small, but in the intention with which you give it.

We do not need to wait for our big opportunity to prove our love for God. We practice it every day in the many little things God gives us to do.

Reflection

What small mundane actions led and prepared you to achieve great things in your life? How can you apply that to preparing for sanctity?

Time For Prayer

Prayer to Faithfully Serve God

Father in Heaven, ever-living source of all that is good, keep me faithful in serving You.

Help me to drink of Christ's Truth, and fill my heart with His Love so that I may serve You in faith and love and reach eternal life.

In the Sacrament of the Eucharist You give me the joy of sharing Your Life. Keep me in Your presence. Let me never be separated from You and help me to do Your Will.

How Can I Find Joy in Suffering?

Small acts of kindness are all well and good for the ordinary upstanding citizen. But saintly holiness requires big heroic acts...and suffering through seemingly insurmountable circumstances. Doesn't it?

The answer to that question has been addressed by many saints. As Teresa of Ávila was known to say, "Trifles make for holiness, but holiness is no trifle."

The essence of the matter is that life here on earth—the purpose of our very existence—is the pursuit of sanctity. Whether we achieve that by doing a million small daily actions with great love or by accomplishing one heroic action that would escalate us to heights that only one in a million persons achieve—it matters not. The point is that we seek holiness and entrust ourselves entirely to God. He will find a way for getting us to heaven if we agree to diligently follow the path He sets before us. Let us consider seven basic steps to holiness.

1. Become childlike. Lord Jesus put a condition on entering heaven: "Truly I say to you, unless you are converted and become like children, you will not enter the kingdom of heaven" (Matthew 18:3). God is our Father, and we must approach Him as loving children—with humility, respect, and trust. We humbly submit our own will to His, saying, Lord, I might disagree with You regarding Your commandments and the Church's doctrines, but I respect that Your ways will lead me to become a better person and I trust that following Your plan will bring me closer to happiness with You.

2. Love the Eucharist Christ. A love for the Eucharistic Lord is one of the true marks of sainthood. Jesus is truly present with us in the Holy Eucharist, during every Mass, in all the tabernacles throughout the world, and through perpetual adoration increasingly offered by many parishes today. We adore Christ in His Holy Presence and are strengthened by His graces to diligently complete our duties with love. We tenderly approach the Eucharistic Lord, saying, 'Lord, I believe. Help my unbelief' (Matthew 9:24).

3. Devote yourself to Jesus's Mother. The second true mark of sanctity is devotion to Mary, the Blessed Mother of God. With His dying breaths, Jesus entrusted us to her, saying, "Behold your mother" (John 19:27). This plea signified more than the concern of an only son for his widowed mother. He asked His beloved disciple—and by extension, all of humanity—to care for the Blessed Mother and treat her with the dignity and respect that Jesus Himself gave. She is revered through various titles by peoples throughout the world. The Catechism of the Catholic Church acknowledges that Mary may be properly invoked as Advocate, Helper, Benefactress, and Mediatrix (CCC 969).

4. Offer extraordinary service in ordinary tasks. Therese of Lisieux, proponent of "The Little Way" astounded generations of faithful by achieving celestial heights in her spiritual life while living a short twenty-four years. Her secret consisted of attending to the tasks of her daily routine with perfection and devotion. She completed all chores as if doing them for Christ and treated all persons as Christ Himself. This very simple attitude may be practiced by us all in any duty we are given.

5. Embrace life's trials. We live in an age where trial is treated as a four-letter word. In a society that idolizes comfort and ease, carrying one's cross and

offering the suffering as a sacrifice seems irrational or even deranged. Yet that is precisely what Christ instructs us to do when we ask for the path to true happiness: 'Whoever wants to be my disciple must deny themselves and take up their cross and follow me' (Matthew 16:24). To advance in holiness, a person need not dig up crosses. However, when those trials come, we pray for the strength to handle the difficulties with equanimity and dignity. We strive to avoid complaint or blame or self-pity. Offer all the God, asking, Lord, share this struggle with me. For You have said, 'My yoke is easy and My burden light.' Walk with me through this trial that I may see the glory You have in store for me.

6. Desire God's smile. As humans, we thrive on bringing smiles to other people's faces. People we love, people we like, people we simply pass in the grocery store—we enjoy seeing them smile. We appreciate when people make us smile. The world becomes a brighter, happier place when we smile and the people around us are smiling as well. If we set our hearts on making God smile, then we approach our days with an attitude that is most pleasing to our heavenly Father.

7. Laugh and trust. Peace, calm, contentment, and acceptance of God's will are all necessary for genuine joy. Joy arises from the deep certainty that

God is in charge and that He is greater than any adversity we may face in this life. Laughter stems from the freedom in knowing that the fate of the world is not entirely up to me or you. God has already won the great battle against Death itself. We still suffer and we continue to work for the salvation of souls. Yet our spirits are at peace knowing that Christ is on our side when we unite ourselves to Him, and He will be victorious.

What Do the Saints Say?

ST. Therese of Lisieux explained that the Lord views our offerings in light of the depth of our love.

You know well enough that Our Lord does not look so much at the greatness of our actions, nor even at their difficulty, but at the love with which we do them.... Our Lord needs from us neither great deeds nor profound thoughts. Neither intelligence nor talents. He cherishes simplicity.

Greatness can flow from simplicity. The Lord loves simplicity of heart.

Reflection

In what ways can you simplify your life to focus on completing your duties with greater love?

Time For Prayer
<u>Prayer For Simplicity</u>

Dear heavenly Father, Even the greatest works are but a tiny moment, a speck in Your universal plan. Let me see past it all, oh Lord, Give me the Kingdom perspective. Even the smallest things can reveal Your great love.

So let me love when I serve a bowl of soup, guck my child into bed, bring home a paycheck, keep my home in order, or visit a sick friend—even just letting someone else go first. These tiny things, oh Lord, reveal You grace and glory. Simplify my life, oh loving Father. Let me not be hurried.

The unnoticed acts of humility, service and love, are bricks that build Your Kingdom. A hug, a call, a cup of coffee can be the first step that helps save a soul. Show me how, my Lord. Guide me as part of the Body of Christ, building Your Kingdom day by day, brick by brick, prayer by prayer.

In Jesus' name, Amen.

10 SAINTLY PRACTICES

- *How Should I Protect Myself Against Evil?*
- *How May I Obtain Daily Grace?*
- *What Can I Do to Console the Sacred Heart of Jesus?*

When we think of saintly practices, we might envision a hermit praying for hours a day, wearing a hair shirt and living on little more than wild honey. The regular devotions of many saints can be quite intimidating.

The great richness of the Catholic Church is that she offers a multitude of devotions and sacramentals in order to ward off evil, procure graces, and participate in Christ's salvific work. This is evident through the wide variety of religious orders which each emphasize a unique aspect of God's love and desire to serve the world. Laypersons are equally encouraged to live out God's call in a dedicated fashion. We are all called to holiness. Sometimes it can be difficult to know where to begin. The important thing is that we begin with one small practice, and we begin today.

How Should I Protect Myself Against Evil?

In order to progress along the path toward virtue, we must necessarily abandon the path toward vice. A person trying to follow both paths simultaneously, with one foot here and the other elsewhere will eventually split in two! As

Christ proclaimed: "No man can serve two masters: for either he will hate the one, and love the other; or else he will hold to the one, and despise the other" (Matthew 6:24). There will come a point in which we must choose.

So, we begin with the easiest action. We begin by shunning evil. We do this to protect ourselves from temptation, to preserve ourselves for the Lord, and ultimately to show our love for Christ. The Catholic Church offers many means of protection, most notably through prayers and sacramentals. Unfortunately, many modern people detest such rituals as remnants of an ancient superstition. Yet, a little research will validate the historical effectiveness of these practices.

We recall that a sacramental provides a material substance signifying a heavenly grace. As with all sacramentals, the power comes by means of the Church's official prayer of blessing, not through the sign itself. The Vatican II document, Sacrosanctum Concilium states:

[W]ell-disposed members of the faithful...are given access to the stream of divine grace which flows from the paschal mystery of the passion, death, the resurrection of Christ, the font from which all sacraments and sacramentals draw their power. There is hardly any proper use of material things which cannot thus be directed toward the sanctification of men and the praise of God (article 61).

Holy water: this blessed water has traditionally been available in every Catholic church as a method for remembering one's baptism. It can also be taken in a personal container and sprinkled throughout the house or used to bless family members or those visiting the home. Holy water has the power to ward off evil spirits. Saint Teresa of Avila described the effect after an experience she had while praying in the convent chapel: "There was some holy water there, and I threw it in that direction; [the devil] never returned again...I often experience that there is nothing that devils flee from more without returning than holy water."

If a splash of holy water can scare off demons, imagine how effective it can be to assist in overcoming temptations as well. Blessing ourselves with holy water gives us spiritual strength to choose the good. We may also use holy water when we are feeling ill or to protect ourselves from future sickness. We may bless ourselves before we embark on a taxing journey or before we enter a hazardous environment.

Blessed salt: This holy mineral developed as a symbol of preservation and spiritual incorruptibility. As a component of the sacrificial meal, salt soon became a symbol of friendship and hospitality. Christ proclaimed, "Salt is good, but if the salt has lost its saltiness, how will you make it salty again? Have salt in yourself, and be at peace with one another" (Mark 9:50). In other words, we must preserve our beliefs with acts of virtue; we must have a savory faith which appeals to others. If our faith is bland, we do not serve to promote God's Kingdom. Blessed salt may be sprinkled around the perimeter of a home or within the house to ward off evil. It may also be used in cooking to practically and spiritually purify food.

Saint Michael Prayer: Pope Leo XIII wrote this powerful recitation in 1884 after experiencing a terrifying vision of the battle between Saint Michael and Satan who vowed to destroy the Church. Saint Michael is specially charged as a fierce protector of the Church and has been assigned to fight evil, to protect faithful souls from the pit of hell, and to champion God's people. Pope Leo XIII requested that this special prayer be recited after every Mass throughout the world. Although this prudent practice is no longer standard, in 1994 Pope Saint John Paul II urged the faithful to continue reciting the prayer after Mass and whenever we desire special protection in precarious circumstances.

What Do the Saints Say?

ST. FULTON SHEEN OF PEORIA, USA detailed the proper position Christians should take against evil.

Christian love bears evil, but it does not tolerate it. It does penance for the sins of others, but it is not broadminded about sin. Real love involves real hatred: whoever has lost the power of moral indignation and the urge to drive the sellers from the temples has also lost a living, fervent love of Truth.

To be zealous for the things of heaven—clarity, harmony, love, truth, light, and life—is to be zealous against the things that are not of heaven—confusion, chaos, apathy, lies, darkness, and death.

Reflection

How may we bring more of the things of heaven into our daily routine? What can we do to minimize the things around us that are not of heaven?

Time For Prayer

Prayer To St. Michael the Archangel

St. Michael the Archangel, defend us in battle, be our protection against the wickedness and snares of the devil. May God rebuke him we humbly pray; and do thou, O Prince of the Heavenly host, by the power of God, cast into hell Satan and all the evil spirits who prowl about the world seeking the ruin of souls.

Amen.

How May I Obtain Daily Grace?

The Miraculous Medal: This medal "designed by the Blessed Mother herself" was originally known as the Medal of the Immaculate Conception. It came to be known as the Miraculous Medal after those who wore it and recited its prayer attributed to it numerous healings, conversions, and other miraculous acts. The medal's images are said to have been requested by Mother Mary when she appeared to the French nun, Catherine Laboure in 1830. Saint Catherine recounted that she saw Mary surrounded by an oval frame engraved with the words: O Mary conceived without sin, pray for us who have recourse to Thee.

The frame rotated, revealing the reverse side which showed the letter M topped with a cross, encircled by 12 stars, and beneath it were the Sacred Heart of Jesus and Immaculate Heart of Mary. Saint Catherine heard the voice of Our Lady instructing, "Have a medal struck upon this model. All those who wear it, when it is blessed, will receive great graces, especially if they wear it round the neck." The holy nun added that the Blessed Mother would protect those who repeated the prayer on the frame, and many graces would be bestowed on those who believed.

The Scapular: We may wear this badge of devotion as a sign of belonging to Jesus and Mary. The Scapular garment reminds us to clothe ourselves in holiness and behave as a child of the Most High God. We wear it as a continuous prayer and proclamation that we are reserved for Heaven. The Scapular is not a good-luck charm but rather a constant reminder to choose the righteous path. This recollection keeps us in the proper mindset and empowers us against temptations.

Blessed candles: these peaceful lights may be used for a duration of time to sanctify an area and recall holy things. Blessed candles are often used in liturgical processions or evening prayer ceremonies. We may also light a blessed candle at home during a holy day meal or while praying a family rosary. Blessed candles are particularly appropriate during a time of struggle, such as for a woman laboring at home prior to a forthcoming birth or a loved one who is ill and facing imminent death.

What Do the Saints Say?

ST. ELIZABETH ANN SETON OF NEW YORK CITY discussed how we may daily imitate Christ. What was the first rule of our dear Savior's life? You know it was to do his Father's will. Well, then, the first purpose of our daily work is to do the will of God; secondly, to do it in the manner he wills; and thirdly, to do it because it is his will. We know certainly that our God calls us to a holy life. We know that he gives us every grace, every abundant grace; and though we are so weak of ourselves, this grace is able to carry us through every obstacle and difficulty.

Therefore, let us ask for God's grace daily, so that we can fulfill the Father's will for each day He bestows upon us.

Reflection

What tools can we use to regularly remind us of heavenly things?

Time For Prayer
Prayer For Grace

Oh my God, You know my weakness and failings, and that without Your help I can accomplish nothing for the good of souls, my own and others'.

Grant me, therefore, the help of Your grace. Grant it according to my particular needs this day.

Enable me to see the task You will set before me in the daily routine of my life, and help me work hard at my appointed tasks.

Teach me to bear patiently all the trials of suffering or failure that may come to me today.

Amen.

What Can I Do to Console the Sacred Heart of Jesus?

Reflecting on the verse, "I looked for someone to comfort me, but found no one" (Psalm 68:21), Pope Pius XI concluded: "If, because of our future sins, the soul of Christ became sorrowful to the point of death, there is no doubt that from that moment on it receives some consolation from our acts of reparation. So that we can and should, even now, console the Sacred Heart."

Sacred Heart Devotion: The late 17th-century visions given by Jesus to French nun Margaret Mary Alacoque greatly bolstered devotion of His Most Sacred Heart. The Lord pulled aside his garment over his bosom and said, "Behold this Heart that has loved men so much."

We may devote ourselves to Jesus by exposing the Sacred Heart image in a place of honor. This is an image of Jesus revealing his Heart flaming with love for us, pierced by a crown of thorns. Saint Margaret Mary reported that the Lord promised to imprint His love on the hearts of those who would wear this image on their person and would destroy in them all disordered movements.

According to Saint Margaret Mary, Jesus attached 12 promises of blessing to those who would devote themselves to His Sacred Heart. Among these favors are listed "peace in their homes, comfort in all their afflictions, and safe refuge in [their] final moment" in this life.

Sacrifice Beads: Sacrifice beads were promulgated by little Therese of Lisieux as a reminder to offer small acts of love to the Lord. As the story goes, one day an older sister of hers gave Therese a set of ten beads which could be pulled along two strings to keep track of small sacrifices made for love of God. Young Therese would pull a bead each time she postponed a treat or allowed someone to have their way. This practice certainly contributed to building virtuous habits in the young soul who ultimately became a remarkable saint. It can assist us in our journey toward holiness as well.

What Do the Saints Say?

ST. THERESE OF LISIEUX spoke of sacrifice as sustenance for souls.

To the right and to the left, I throw to my little birds the good grain that God places in my hands. And then I let things take their course! I busy myself with it no more. Sometimes, it's just as though I had thrown nothing; at other times, it does some good. But God tells me: "Give, give always, without being concerned with the results."

We are to give without counting the cost and without expecting the reward.

Reflection

What daily tasks can I offer to the Lord as a loving sacrifice?

Time For Prayer

An Act of Consecration to the Sacred Heart of Jesus #1

Oh dear Sacred Heart of Jesus, I give You my whole heart. I see Your Heart on fire for love of me. I want to be in this fiery furnace and know the love of God.

Take me, Jesus. Use me as Your little servant to spread Your love to this world. I give myself entirely to You and I ask the Holy Spirit to make me more like You.

I want to be a little child of the Father. I give You my heart, keep me in Your Heart and teach me Your way of love. Amen.

COLLECTION

OF

PRAYERS

ANIMA CHRISTI

Soul of Christ, sanctify me;
Body of Christ, save me;
Blood of Christ, inebriate me;
Water from the side of Christ, wash me;
Passion of Christ, strengthen me;
O good Jesus hear me;
Within your wounds hide me;
separated from you, let me never be;
From the evil one protect me;
At the hour of my death, call me;
And close to you bid me; That with your saints,
I may be praising you forever and ever.

THE DIVINE PRAISES

Blessed be God.
Blessed be His Holy Name.
Blessed be Jesus Christ, true God and true Man.
Blessed be the Name of Jesus.
Blessed be His Most Sacred Heart.
Blessed be His Most Precious Blood.
Blessed be Jesus in the Most Holy Sacrament of the Altar.

Blessed be the Holy Spirit, the Paraclete.
Blessed be the great Mother of God, Mary
most Holy.
Blessed be her Holy and Immaculate
Conception.
Blessed be her Glorious Assumption.
Blessed be the name of Mary, Virgin and
Mother.
Blessed be St. Joseph, her most chaste spouse.
Blessed be God in His Angels and in His
Saints.

HAIL TO THEE, TRUE BODY (A Prayer to our Eucharistic Lord)

Hail to thee, true body born
From Virgin Mary's womb!
The same that on the cross was nailed
And bore for man the bitter doom.

Thou, whose side was pierced and flowed
Both with water and with blood;
Suffer us to taste of thee,
In our life's last agony.

O kind, O loving one!
O sweet Jesus, Mary's Son!

ST. JOHN VIANNEY PRAYER

> O my God, come to me, so that You may
> dwell in me and I may dwell in You.

SHORT PRAYER AFTER COMMUNION

> Sweetest Jesus,
> Body and Blood most Holy,
> be the delight and pleasure of my soul,
> my strength and salvation in all temptations,
> my joy and peace in every trial,
> my light and guide in every word and deed,
> and my final protection in death. Amen.

A SHORT ADORATION PRAYER BEFORE MEDITATION

> I place myself in the presence of Him, in
> whose Incarnate Presence I am before. I
> place myself there.

> I adore Thee, O my Savior, present here as
> God and man, in soul and body, in true
> flesh and blood.

I acknowledge and confess that I kneel before that Sacred Humanity, which was conceived in Mary's womb and lay in Mary's bosom; which grew up to man's estate, and by the Sea of Galilee called the Twelve, wrought miracles, and spoke words of wisdom and peace; which in due season hung on the cross, lay in the tomb, rose from the dead, and now reigns in heaven.

I praise, and bless, and give myself wholly to Him, Who is the true Bread of my soul, and my everlasting joy.

FATIMA ANGEL'S PRAYER (Given by an angel to the children of Fatima)

O Most Holy Trinity, Father, Son and Holy Spirit, I adore Thee profoundly.

I offer Thee the most precious Body, Blood, Soul and Divinity of Jesus Christ, present in all the tabernacles of the world, in reparation for the outrages, sacrileges and indifference by which He is offended.

By the infinite merits of the Sacred Heart of
Jesus and the Immaculate Heart of Mary, I
beg the conversion of poor sinners.

PRAYER BEFORE CONFESSION

O Holy Spirit. Source of all light, Spirit of
wisdom, of understanding, and of
knowledge, come to my assistance and
enable me to make a good confession.
Enlighten me and help me now to know my
sins as one day I shall be forced to
recognize them before Thy judgment seat.
Bring to my mind the evil which I have done
and the good which I have neglected.
Permit me not to be blinded by self-love.
Grant me, moreover, heartfelt sorrow for my
transgressions, and the grace of a sincere
confession, so that I may be forgiven and
admitted into Thy friendship.

ACT OF CONTRITION

O my God, I am heartily sorry for having
offended Thee. And I detest all my sins

because I dread the loss of heaven and the pains of hell, but most of all because they offend Thee, my God, Who art all good and deserving of all my love.

I firmly resolve, with the help of Thy grace, to confess my sins, to do penance, and to amend my life. Amen.

REPENTANCE PRAYER

Dear God, I come to You as a sinner who is undeserving of your grace and presence. I repent all my sins and ask You to forgive me so that my request may be heard by You.

Lord, have mercy on me and fill me with Your grace. Wash me with the blood of Your son, Jesus Christ, that I may shine and walk unashamed.

I ask for Your favor from this moment to the end of the day. I thank You, for You are faithful. Amen

HAIL HOLY QUEEN

Hail, holy Queen, Mother of mercy, our life, our sweetness and our hope.

To thee do we cry, poor banished children of Eve.

To thee to we send up our sighs, mourning and weeping in this valley of tears.

Turn, then, most gracious advocate, thine eyes of mercy toward us; and after this, our exile, show unto us the blessed fruit of thy womb, Jesus.

O clement, O loving, O sweet Virgin Mary:

V. Pray for us, O holy Mother of God,

R. That we may be made worthy of the promises of Christ.

Let us pray.

O God, whose only-begotten Son, by His life, death and resurrection, has purchased for us the rewards of eternal life, grant, we beseech Thee, that meditating on these mysteries of the most holy Rosary of the

Blessed Virgin Mary, we may imitate what they contain, and obtain what they promise, through the same Christ our Lord. Amen.

CATHOLIC MORNING PRAYER

O Jesus, through the Immaculate Heart of Mary, I offer you my prayers, works, joys, and sufferings of this day for all the intentions of you Sacred Heart, in union with the holy sacrifice of the Mass throughout the world, in thanksgiving for your favors, in reparation for my sins, for the intentions of all my associates, and especially for the intentions of our Holy Father, the Pope. Amen.

CLOSING PRAYER FOR DIVING MERCY CHAPLET (optional)

Eternal God, in whom mercy is endless and the treasury of compassion inexhaustible, look kindly upon us and increase Your mercy in us, that in difficult moments we might not despair nor become despondent, but with

great confidence submit ourselves to Your
holy will, which is Love and Mercy itself.

COME, HOLY SPIRIT

Come Holy Spirit, fill the hearts of your
faithful and kindle in them the fire of
your love. Send forth your Spirit and they
shall be created. And You shall renew the
face of the earth.

O, God, who by the light of the Holy Spirit,
did instruct the hearts of the faithful,
grant that by the same Holy Spirit we
may be truly wise and ever enjoy His
consolations, Through Christ Our Lord.
Amen.

THE LORD'S PRAYER

Our Father, Who art in heaven, hallowed be
Thy name.

Thy Kingdom come. Thy will be done on
earth, as it is in heaven.

Give us this day our daily bread. And forgive
us our trespasses as we forgive those who
trespass against us.

HAIL MARY

Hail Mary, Full of Grace, the Lord is with you.
Blessed are you among women, and
blessed is the fruit of your womb, Jesus.

Holy Mary, Mother of God, pray for us
sinners now, and at the hour of our death.
Amen.

TEACH US TO LOVE

Lord, we thank Thee for all the love that has
been given to us, for the love of family
and friends, and above all for Your love
poured out upon us every moment of our
lives in steadfast glory.

Forgive our unworthiness. Forgive the many
times we have disappointed those who
love us, have failed them, wearied them,
saddened them.

Failing them we have failed You and hurting
them we have wounded our Savior
who for love's sake died for us. Lord, have
mercy on us, and forgive.

You do not fail those who love you. You do
not change nor vary. Teach us Your own
constancy in love, Your humility,
selflessness and generosity.

Look in pity on our small and tarnished
loving, protect, foster and strengthen it,
that it may be less unworthy to be offered
to You and to Your children. O Light of
the World, teach us how to love. Amen.

RECOMMENDATION TO THE SACRED HEART OF JESUS

O Sweetest Heart of Jesus, to Thee I commend
my body and my soul this night, that they
may calmly rest in Thee. And as I cannot
praise my God while I sleep, do Thou deign to
supply my lack of service, and for every
beating of my heart give praise to the most
Holy Trinity on my behalf; receive into
Thyself every breath I draw, and offer them

all to God as glowing sparks of Divine love.
Amen.

A PRAYER FOR KINDNESS IN ALL THINGS

Dear Lord, I praise You as the essence of all
things loving. You are complete in
Yourself. You are unconditional in Love.

In my heart I desire to be more like You, and I
invite You to be with me as I move about
through my day. When I begin to
compare myself to others, let me
remember that we are all made in Your
likeness, and that each of our bodies is a
temple of Your Holy Spirit.

When I am tempted to make judgments
about the actions, behaviors, or even the
looks of others as a way of making myself
feel better, come to my aid and bring
about in me a spirit of contentment, a
spirit of gratitude.

Help me to treat each person I encounter as I
would like to be treated and fill me with
loving kindness so that my thoughts,

words, and deeds flow from Your Spirit of
unconditional Love.

Let me remember You always. Let me be ever
aware of Your presence in each moment
of my life, as I would surely cease to live,
to move, to have my being if thought of
me falls from Your mind's embrace for
the span of even one breath; for it is Your
breath that gives me life.

I ask all these things through Christ who
strengthens me. Amen.

PRAYER FOR A SPIRIT OF SERVICE

Dear loving Lord, You sent Your Son to serve.
You sent Him to give His life for me. Let
Your Spirit awaken in me the same spirit
of service.
Let me not look for position or gain. Instead,
show me how to let others go before me.
Make me meek, make me humble so I too can
give my life—willfully, obediently, and
faithfully—even when it hurts, in love,
with Christ, and like Christ. In Jesus'
name. Amen.

PRAYER TO SERVE GOD WITH LOVE

Lord, help us to follow the example of saints
who have gone before so that we may
serve You with love and obtain perfect
joy.

We ask this through our Lord Jesus Christ,
who lives and reigns with you and the
Holy Spirit, one God, forever and ever.
Amen.

A PRAYER FOR THE GRACE TO FORGIVE

Dear Lord, I come to You with a heart that is
heavy with resentment. The hurt I carry
with me is taking its toll, slowly closing
the door of my heart to love.

I have been unjustly hurt and I don't want to
forgive, yet, I beg you to grant me the
grace to forgive the one who has hurt me,
even though the very thought of doing so
is painful to me.

Turn my eyes now to You and show me Your
wounds. Show me Your bloody face. Show
me Your torn flesh.

Help me to always remember that You are
the True Victim who was suffered the
most unjust hurt ever known to
humankind.

Give me the grace to be sorrowful for my sins
that nailed You to the cross and whisper
in my ear Your loving words, "Father
forgive them for they know not what they
do."

With Your tenderness, O Lord, I know my
heart will melt and be filled with Your
love, that I may forgive my offender.
Amen.

PRAYER FOR COURAGE

Lord, give me courage in my everyday
life. Courage to speak Your truth and to
defend the faith. Courage to follow Your
commandments and to live
Your beatitudes.

Courage to live a moral life, even if it means
losing friends. Courage to pray. Courage to
love others, especially the poor. Courage
to visit the sick and the lonely.

Lord, may I not fall back in fear, but may I do
Your will, strengthened by Your love.

PRAYER FOR THE NEW EVANGELIZATION

Heavenly Father, pour forth Your Holy Spirit
to inspire me with these words from Holy
Scripture.

Stir in my soul the desire to renew my faith
and deepen my relationship with your
Son, our Lord Jesus Christ, so that I might
truly believe in and live the Good News.

Open my heart to hear the Gospel and grant
me the confidence to proclaim the Good
News to others.

Pour out your Spirit, so that I might be
strengthened to go forth and witness to
the Gospel in my everyday life through
my words and actions.

ETERNAL GOD (By St. Francis Xavier S.J.)

Eternal God, Creator of all things, remember that You alone have created the souls of unbelievers, which You have made according to Your image and likeness.

Behold, O Lord, how to Your dishonor, many of them are falling into Hell.

Remember, O Lord, Your Son Jesus Christ, who so generously shed His Blood and suffered for them.

Do not permit that Your Son, Our Lord, remain unknown by unbelievers, but, with the help of Your Saints and the Church, the Bride of Your Son, remember Your mercy.

Forget their idolatry and infidelity, and make them know Him, whom You have sent, Jesus Christ, Your Son, Our Lord, who is our salvation, our life and our resurrection, through whom we have been saved and redeemed, and to whom is due glory forever. Amen.

PRAYER FOR VISION AND INSTRUCTION

Dear God, We pray that You would remind us that that we are all a part of building and expanding Your Kingdom. We ask that you give us a fresh vision for Your purpose for our lives.

We ask that You open our eyes, our ears, our hearts, and our minds to your vision so that we can live out our purpose. Remove anything from our lives that hinders us from discerning Your vision.

We pray that You would draw us closer to You as you bring us revelation to our purpose. Please reveal to us what we need to do today to not run wild, but rather be focused on Your divine vision. In Jesus' Name, Amen.

PRAYER TO BE THE GENUINE ARTICLE

Dear God, I want to be the genuine article. I don't want to be watered down. Diluted.

I want Your strong and pure love to come through me in a genuine way. Genuine love coming through me in a way that

will bless others. With a divine sincerity—
nothing fake.

I pray to become a better person by allowing
love to freely flow through me without
restriction. Without alteration. As genuine
as You are, dear God. Amen.

PRAYER TO FIND THE RIGHT PATH (by Thomas Merton)

My Lord God, I have no idea where I am
going. I do not see the road ahead of me. I
cannot know for certain where it will end.
Nor do I really know myself, and the fact
that I think I am following Your will does
not mean that I am actually doing so.
But I believe that the desire to please You does
in fact please You. And I hope I have that
desire in all that I am doing. I hope that I
will never do anything apart from that
desire. And I know that if I do this You
will lead me by the right road, though I
may know nothing about it.
Therefore, I will trust You always though I
may seem to be lost and in the shadow of
death. I will not fear, for You are ever with

me, and You will never leave me to face
my perils alone.

PRAYER FOR CONFIDENCE IN THE REVEALED PURPOSE

Dear God, Thank You that even if what we
see in front of us doesn't feel good or look
good, Your plans are good. That even if
harm comes our way, You'll use it for
good.

Thank You for the hope we can find in You.
We trust that You have our future
planned out from the very beginning.
Allow us to rest in You and rest in Your
master plan.

Give us the confidence that You have nothing
but good planned for us. Remind us that
even though we don't know the full plan,
that You know the plan. May we lean into
You. In Jesus' Name, Amen.

PENTECOST PRAYER

O Holy Spirit, divine Spirit of light and love, I
consecrate to You my understanding, my
heart, my will, my whole being for time
and for eternity.

May my understanding always be submissive
to Your heavenly inspirations and to the
teachings of the Holy Catholic Church, of
which You are the infallible Guide.

May my heart ever be inflamed with love of
God and of my neighbor.

May my will always conform to the divine
will, and may my whole life be a faithful
imitation of the life and virtues of our
Lord and Savior Jesus Christ, to whom be
honor and glory forever. Amen.

PRAYER FOR THE CHURCH #3

O God! our refuge and our strength, look
down with favor on Thy people who cry to
Thee; and through the intercession of the
glorious and Immaculate Virgin Mary,
Mother of God, of Saint Joseph her Spouse, of
Thy blessed Apostles Peter and Paul, and of

all the Saints, in mercy and goodness hear our prayers for the conversion of sinners, and for the liberty and exaltation of our holy Mother the Church. Through the same Christ our Lord. Amen.

PRAYER FOR A NEW CREATION

Jesus, thank you for not wanting to just fix our lives but make of us a 'new creation.'

Holy Spirit, we ask You to show us the beauty of the life You have planned for us.

We give You this time together and ask for the grace to share openly and allow our hearts and minds to be transformed by Your love. Amen.

A PRAYER FOR DEVOTED LAITY IN THE CHURCH

O Lord, our God, You called Your people to be Your Church. As they gather together in Your Name, may they love, honor, and

follow Your Son to eternal life in the
Kingdom He promised.

Let their worship always be sincere, and help
them to find Your saving Love in the
Church and its Sacraments.

Fill with the Spirit of Christ those whom You
call to live in the midst of the world and
its concern. Help them by their work on
earth to build up Your eternal Kingdom.
May they be effective witnesses to the
Truth of the Gospel and make Your
Church a living presence in the midst of
the world.

Increase the gifts You have given Your
Church that Your faithful people may
continue to grow in holiness and in
imitation of Your Beloved Son

PRAYER FOR HOLINESS

Breathe in me,
O Holy Spirit,
that my thoughts may all be holy.

Act in me,
O Holy Spirit,
that my work, too, may be holy.

Draw my heart,
 O Holy Spirit,
  that I love only what is holy.

Strengthen me,
 O Holy Spirit,
  to defend all that is holy.

Guard me so,
 O Holy Spirit,
  that I may always be holy.

Amen.

PRAYER TO FAITHFULLY SERVE GOD

Father in Heaven, ever-living source of all that is good, keep me faithful in serving You.

Help me to drink of Christ's Truth, and fill my heart with His Love so that I may serve You in faith and love and reach eternal life.

In the Sacrament of the Eucharist You give me the joy of sharing Your Life. Keep me in Your presence. Let me never be separated from You and help me to do Your Will.

PRAYER FOR SIMPLICITY

Dear heavenly Father, Even the greatest works are but a tiny moment, a speck in Your universal plan. Let me see past it all, oh Lord, Give me the Kingdom perspective. Even the smallest things can reveal Your great love.

So let me love when I serve a bowl of soup, guck my child into bed, bring home a paycheck, keep my home in order, or visit a sick friend—even just letting someone else go first. These tiny things, oh Lord, reveal You grace and glory. Simplify my life, oh loving Father. Let me not be hurried.

The unnoticed acts of humility, service and love, are bricks that build Your Kingdom. A hug, a call, a cup of coffee can be the first step that helps save a soul. Show me how, my Lord. Guide me as part of the Body of Christ, building Your Kingdom day by day, brick by brick, prayer by prayer. In Jesus' name, Amen.

PRAYER TO ST. MICHAEL THE ARCHANGEL

St. Michael the Archangel, defend us in battle, be our protection against the wickedness and snares of the devil. May God rebuke him we humbly pray; and do thou, O Prince of the Heavenly host, by the power of God, cast into

hell Satan and all the evil spirits who prowl
about the world seeking the ruin of souls.
Amen

PRAYER FOR GRACE

Oh my God, You know my weakness and
   failings, and that without Your help I can
   accomplish nothing for the good of souls,
   my own and others'.
Grant me, therefore, the help of Your grace.
   Grant it according to my particular needs
   this day.
Enable me to see the task You will set before
   me in the daily routine of my life, and
   help me work hard at my appointed tasks.
Teach me to bear patiently all the trials of
   suffering or failure that may come to me
   today. Amen.

AN ACT OF CONSECRATION TO THE SACRED HEART OF JESUS # 1

Oh dear Sacred Heart of Jesus, I give You my whole heart. I see Your Heart on fire for love of me. I want to be in this fiery furnace and know the love of God.

Take me, Jesus. Use me as Your little servant to spread Your love to this world. I give myself entirely to You and I ask the Holy Spirit to make me more like You.

I want to be a little child of the Father. I give You my heart, keep me in Your Heart and teach me Your way of love. Amen.

ABOUT THE AUTHORS

Jose Licea was born and raised in the Los Angeles metropolitan area of southern California. He moved with his family to the central valley of California in his younger years where he met his beautiful wife, Dalia Licea. Jose considers his Catholic faith and family to be of the utmost importance to him. If he isn't spending time with his family, you can almost always find him studying Catholic apologetics or producing Catholic music. In Communion With Christ is Jose's first book.

Dalia Licea was born in Anchorage, Alaska and was raised in the central valley of California where she met her wonderful husband, Jose Licea. Dalia considers her Catholic faith and family to be of the utmost importance to her. If she isn't spending time with her family, you can almost always find her reading, writing, creating art, rosaries, and jewelry. In Communion With Christ is Dalia's first book.

If you would like to contact the authors, you may do so by visiting ChristianCatholicMedia.com.

Made in the USA
Monee, IL
23 August 2022

11903323R10100